Philosophy
for Kids

Philosophy for Kids

40 Fun Questions That Help You Wonder . . . About Everything!

David A. White, Ph.D.

Illustrations by Cheryle Chapline

Routledge
Taylor & Francis Group

NEW YORK AND LONDON

First published in 2001 by Prufrock Press Inc.

Published in 2021 by Routledge
605 Third Avenue, New York, NY 10017
2 Park Square, Milton Park, Abingdon, Oxon OX14 4RN

Routledge is an imprint of the Taylor & Francis Group, an informa business

Copyright © 2001 by Taylor & Francis Group

Cover and layout design by James Kendrick
Cover Art: Raphael, The School of Athens (Scala/Art Resource, New York)

ISBN: 9781032143705 (hbk)
ISBN: 9781882664702 (pbk)

DOI: 10.4324/9781003237150

Dedication

First, to the many young people whose enthusiasm and energy have allowed me the unique privilege of feeling the fire and sensing the vision of their thinking on the fundamental issues of philosophy. And second, to all the teachers who have been so gracious and cooperative in sharing their classrooms and their experience.

Philosophy for Kids

All lessons in this book align to the following standards.

Cluster	Common Core State Standards in ELA-Literacy
College and Career Readiness Anchor Standards for Reading (K-12)	CCRA.R.1 Read closely to determine what the text says explicitly and to make logical inferences from it; cite specific textual evidence when writing or speaking to support conclusions drawn from the text. CCRA.R.2 Determine central ideas or themes of a text and analyze their development; summarize the key supporting details and ideas. CCRA.R.3 Analyze how and why individuals, events, or ideas develop and interact over the course of a text. CCRA.R.8 Delineate and evaluate the argument and specific claims in a text, including the validity of the reasoning as well as the relevance and sufficiency of the evidence. CCRA.R.10 Read and comprehend complex literary and informational texts independently and proficiently.
College and Career Readiness Anchor Standards for Speaking and Listening (K-12)	CCRA.SL.1 Prepare for and participate effectively in a range of conversations and collaborations with diverse partners, building on others' ideas and expressing their own clearly and persuasively.
College and Career Readiness Anchor Standards for Language (K-12)	CCRA.L.4 Determine or clarify the meaning of unknown and multiple-meaning words and phrases by using context clues, analyzing meaningful word parts, and consulting general and specialized reference materials, as appropriate. CCRA.L.6 Acquire and use accurately a range of general academic and domain-specific words and phrases sufficient for reading, writing, speaking, and listening at the college and career readiness level; demonstrate independence in gathering vocabulary knowledge when encountering an unknown term important to comprehension or expression.

Table of Contents

Part III—Reality   65

Part IV—Critical Thinking   97

Preface

*I*n 1993, after many years teaching philosophy in colleges and universities—frequently to jaded and unresponsive audiences—I began giving programs in primary-source philosophy to elementary school students in Chicago schools, grades 6–8, and also to high school students. These programs were sponsored by the Chicago Public Schools. Since 1993, I have also presented a variety of philosophy courses in grades 4–9 for Northwestern University's Center for Talent Development.

These programs consist primarily of analyzing brief passages from important philosophers throughout the history of the discipline—punctuated by considerable interaction between me and the students. Simply put, we argue a lot. In fact, a treasured memory is the comment of an especially contentious (and perceptive) sixth grader who one day stopped en route to his next class and said, with great gusto: *"I really like philosophy; it's the only class where we get rewarded for arguing!"*

These youthful audiences were neither jaded nor unresponsive. Indeed, my overwhelming reaction after the seven years (and counting) I have spent philosophizing with young people is that they are very thoughtful about important issues. If appropriate topics are suitably presented, young people do wonderful things with these ideas. They love to think about such questions, to express their thoughts and to argue about their views—often with great intensity and insight. This interest is reflected in how I am occasionally greeted—*"Hey, philosophy dude!"* I am in no sense a "dude," but the fact that students think of me in this way suggests that for them it is "cool" to do philosophy in the classroom.

Philosophy for Kids opens the door to the cool way philosophers wonder about the world through a format combining the precision of philosophical thought with a light and, at times, loony touch. Anyone 10 or over is invited to browse through this book and participate in thoughtful activities evoking the wondrous world of philosophical ideas. My public hope is that thinking about these questions will prove exciting, informative, and fun. My private hope is that, once this excitement thrills their minds, young people will start reading about philosophical questions on their own. Such a response would realize a philosophy teacher's dream!

Acknowledgments

Many people contributed to the genesis and final form of this book and I would like to thank them: Linda Klawitter, who once upon a time urged me to direct my experiences with young people and philosophy into the written word; Lisa Leonard, who first suggested the idea of a "fun" book on philosophy for kids; the teachers and administrators who participated in the field testing of *Philosophy for Kids* and made a number of useful suggestions for improving both the content and design of the work; Gillian Barr, Elena Crushshon, Stephanie Daczyszyn, James Heller, Linda Klawitter, Mark Klein, Luba Markewycz, Suzanne Ranalli, Suzanne Saposnik, Sheila Schlaggar, Cynthia Sprague, Charlotte Stiritz, and JoAnna Theodore.

Special thanks go to Dr. James Delisle, who took time from his indefatigable labors on behalf of gifted students everywhere to read and evaluate the text and to use it with students and student teachers; Dr. Jennifer Thompson, who incorporated her own experience in teaching philosophy to gifted students and her keen sense of clarity and philosophical rigor into many valuable comments and suggestions; Dr. Judith Stoffel, who did not allow her inescapable destiny as my sister to interfere with the ability to draw on her considerable experience with young people's literature for purposes of offering a host of useful suggestions and critical comments on the text, as well as providing assistance with the bibliography; Lydia Rossi and Manya Treece for their gifts in combining philosophical rigor with visual art (and humor!). And a sincere "thank you" to Joel McIntosh of Prufrock Press, whose interest in the idea of this book, suggestions for organization, and efforts to see the final product into the world were an inspiration throughout the process of production.

Closer to home, I want to thank Daniel and Colin White for their stoical patience and assistance in dealing with my studied inexpertise with the computer and also Mary Jeanne Larrabee for many kindnesses, both large and small, in helping to produce the manuscript in its final form.

Introduction

About This Book

The ancient Greeks believed that philosophy begins with wonder. If this belief is true, then young people should make excellent philosophers since they naturally wonder about many things. If you have ever wondered about why you felt a certain way when things happen to you, or why animals or plants do what they do, or why stars shine at night, or why a machine works, then you might be a philosopher.

Philosophy for Kids is intended to foster that sense of wonder and to aim it in many directions. The word *philosophy* was coined by the Greeks and it means "love of wisdom." A philosopher is not necessarily wise, but a philosopher wants to *become* wise. Wise about what? In the traditional sense of philosophy, wise about everything—yourself, the people around you, the world you live in.

For example, have you ever wondered whether someone who you thought was your friend is really your friend? Have you ever wondered about what time is, which is a very different question from "*What time is it?*" Did you ever wonder what happens to numbers when you aren't thinking about them during your math class? Did you know that the answer to the old question about whether a tree makes a sound when it falls in the forest with no one around is very important to philosophy? These are only a few of the ideas you can explore in this book. There are many others equally as interesting.

Philosophers have been thinking about these questions for almost 3,000 years. Philosophers come in all shapes, races, nationalities. They can be men or women, older, middle-aged, younger. Some can even be your age. In this book, you will find 40 questions that philosophers have often asked. Perhaps you've already thought of some of these questions. For example, "*Should you ever tell a lie?*" or "*Can computers think?*" But others will probably be new—"*How do you know for certain that things move?*" or "*Is it possible to think about nothing at all?*" Look over the questions in the Table of Contents and see how many of them you have already asked yourself or, perhaps, someone else. If you find a question that looks interesting, turn to that question in the book. It's time to try philosophy!

When you begin to explore a question, you'll see an introduction briefly explaining it. This discussion is followed by an activity inviting you to think about the question and helping you to learn about it in an interesting and enjoyable way. An important philosopher's answer to the question is included in the

DOI: 10.4324/9781003237150-1

1

discussion so you can see what that individual thought about the question. (The philosopher's name appears at the top of the page.) After you have been introduced to the philosopher's thoughts, there are more questions and activities (in the section called For Further Thought) to help you discover *your own* answer to the question. Also, there is a Glossary at the end of the book to remind you of the meanings of important philosophical words.

It is essential to realize that philosophy is not like mathematics, where answers to problems appear at the back of the book. In fact, philosophers often keep thinking about a question even after they feel they have answered it. Thus, although the discussions and activities in this book are fun, they are also challenging. For example, "*Can you think about nothing at all?*" is a question that might sound easy to answer but, in fact, is not (as the discussion of this question will show). All 40 questions are answered in such a way as to make you want to think even more about them. So, have fun wondering about—and learning—philosophy!

Philosophy and Questioning

If you are reading this, then you are probably curious. If you are curious, then you wonder a lot. If you wonder a lot, then you ask questions. And if you are serious about the questions you ask, then you want answers to your questions.

Philosophy asks questions—lots of them. These questions are about concepts or ideas that concern everyone in one way or another—justice, friendship, time, truth, and so forth. But, the questions are not easily answered because they are about very basic issues and because it is challenging to reason about these issues, as philosophers typically do. In fact, some of the questions are in the form of a paradox—an especially fascinating paradox will present you with a simple three-word sentence and you will be mystified as to whether this sentence is true or false! Another paradox, over 2,000 years old, will make you wonder whether you have ever really seen anything move!

Thinking about all the issues contained in this book will help you to understand them and also, in the process, help you to understand more about yourself. Here are some examples of questions that will increase your self-knowledge: "*Are you a fair and just person?*" "*Should you be rewarded for your effort in school?*" "*Are you the same person you were five years ago?*" Once you begin to start thinking about these and other questions, you will enjoy it. You will learn about all sorts of things and see the value in wanting to be wise. You will be a philosopher.

As you browse through the questions in this book, you will think of many things. You will also notice that one question almost always leads to other questions, some of which will be discussed in other parts of the book. But, many of the new questions you'll discover won't be discussed. The reading list at the end of the book—Additional Reading in Philosophy—should be useful in giving you some hints for where you can go to learn more and to become involved in more thinking and more discussion.

Reading about philosophical ideas is an important source of information, but it is equally important to talk to people about your own thoughts—classmates, friends, family members and, of course, your teachers. Many of the activities are more interesting—and more fun—when done with your friends or classmates. Then you can compare your philosophical ideas and, in the process, match wits with other young philosophers. We can learn a great deal from talking, and listening, to others about philosophical issues. We can also learn a great deal by listening to ourselves as we think about these issues.

Important Things to Remember About the Activities

Philosophy for Kids includes activities in order to help you understand philosophical ideas and to enjoy yourself while doing so. Some of the activities resemble the kind of exercises that many people have done in school: true/false questions, multiple-choice questions, fill in the blanks. However, these activities are *not* tests; they just look like tests so that you will think hard when you answer them. The questions—and answers—are discussed, so you should not consider the activities as homework or as work of any sort. So, keep this element of playfulness in mind when you are doing an activity for a question such as "*Are impossible things ever possible?*" (which is, by the way, a very important philosophical question). Also, many of the activities can be repeated after a time, so it might be a good idea to use a pencil if you want to write your answers in this book.

Some activity questions—and every now and then some of the answers—are a bit silly. This is part of the fun. But, the fun part of philosophy only begins here. The really interesting part of philosophy comes later, when you start to read the writings of the philosophers and think about their ideas on your own and in conversations with others.

When you become fascinated by these questions and activities, you may have a feeling of novelty, or even strangeness, at something you have never thought about before or something you have thought about, but not in the way you are thinking about it now. This feeling is perfectly normal. In fact, it shows that you have been doing very well as a philosopher. Remember that thinking is fun, but also challenging. If you start to wonder about something and then begin to think about it, try to keep thinking until you have increased your understanding of the basic idea. A true philosopher keeps striving to become wise. So, the more you think about and discuss these issues, the more philosophical you will be.

Finally, all the questions contain, here and there, a short saying by a famous (and, occasionally, not so famous) person. These sayings are intended to help you focus your thinking about that question. The sayings often express the point of the question in a vivid or witty way, as a poet or comedian might. However, now and then the saying will challenge the point of the question with another possible way of approaching that question. Also, as you think about the questions, keep in mind the following quotation wherever you explore in *Philosophy for Kids*:

"When a thing is funny, search it for a hidden truth."
George Bernard Shaw, playwright and author

Notes for Teachers and Parents

Philosophy is an ancient and universal discipline. The questions posed in this book receive answers from philosophers who span almost 3,000 years of history and who represent a wide variety of cultures.

Young people will be initially attracted to, and intrigued by, the concrete questions asked. And yet, all these questions are fundamental or closely related to basic issues in philosophy. It is important to keep in mind, however, that many other questions equally fundamental are also well worth considering, and it would be prudent to anticipate that young people will quickly become aware of this feature of philosophy.

Encourage browsing among these questions. It is characteristic of wonder that it can appear at any time and be directed at almost anything. Try not to stifle this precious resource.

It is also characteristic of philosophical questions to exhibit an interlocking effect. Thus, to start on any one question will naturally lead the investigator to a multitude of others. The discussions of each question reflect this feature: In fact, they invite it by making references to other questions that are discussed elsewhere in the book.

It is unlikely that all kids will find each question to be interesting and engaging. This is normal. But what often happens, fascinating and wonderful to behold, is that a student who had been indifferent to philosophy suddenly becomes intrigued by a question and then appreciates the importance of this kind of intellectual endeavor. So, the message here at the outset is to be patient if some students do not find the initial exercises in philosophy to be worthwhile.

A teacher could use *Philosophy for Kids* as a textbook in philosophy by introducing students to some of the questions—and "fun" responses—that philosophers have asked over the centuries. But, *Philosophy for Kids* is not primarily intended as a textbook. It is intended to be fun and philosophical. As a result, a young person can browse through the contents, looking at any of the 40 questions, hopscotching around the book until this or that question prods interest. And then another . . . and another . . . .

A section intended primarily for teachers (and parents) does, however, appear at the end of the book. This section—How To Philosophize If You Are Not a Philosopher—contains discussions intended to facilitate the use of this book: Organization, Classroom Procedures, Question Review and Teaching Tips, and Curricular Integration. This material may be helpful if teachers wish to use *Philosophy for Kids* in a more formal setting in the classroom.

About the Cover

The cover of *Philosophy for Kids* is *The School of Athens*, a fresco in the Vatican Museum by the Italian master Raphael, painted in 1510 and restored in 1996. The figures depict a group of Greek philosophers and mathematicians (as well as several representations of Raphael himself). The two thinkers highlighted in the center are Plato, pointing upward to indicate the true reality is spiritual, and Aristotle, pointing downward to emphasize to his teacher Plato that reality on earth also matters. Socrates stands at Plato's right, looking away in thoughtful conversation. Heraclitus reclines below Plato, with Parmenides close at hand. Zeno is to the far left. All these philosophers appear at various moments in *Philosophy for Kids* (the book Aristotle is holding is the *Nicomachean Ethics*, the source of Question #2 on friendship). This "timeless academy" evokes with beauty and power the historical sweep of philosophical ideas, which is one of the central features *of Philosophy for Kids*.

The author would like to thank Prufrock Press editors Jim and Christy Kendrick for suggesting this cover and also for all their labors in the production of what is, for the author, a book of thoughtful and elegant design duly fitting both its content and its intended audience.

The author of *Philosophy for Kids* would be very interested in hearing reactions of readers, teachers, parents, or young people who have in any way used this book. Please send your comments to him at: dwhite6886@aol.com

This delightful depiction of a typically befuddled philosophy teacher—the author of *Philosophy for Kids*—was done by an eighth grader. Just before the first session of her final year in the philosophy program at her school, she spotted me waiting outside the classroom and commented, "Oh, it's *you*," in a glacial tone intimating that the sight of the philosophy teacher looming on her educational horizon was as exciting as an impending trip to the dentist. Then, sensing that something should be done to preserve a measure of teacher-student goodwill, she added, "Don't take it personally. I just don't like philosophy." Ten weeks later, she presented this drawing to me after the final session of the program. I have managed to convince myself that the quality and wit of this portrait suggest that she did not find the experience of philosophy to be too horribly painful after all.

PART I

Values

What do you think is important? Having fun? Making friends? Getting good grades in school? Learning about things? Being successful? Getting rich? Becoming famous? Helping others? Doing the right thing?

Your values are whatever interests you and whatever you think is important. The subject of values has concerned philosophers since philosophy began. As a result, philosophers have spent much time and effort describing values and explaining why they are important in our lives. The name of this branch of philosophy is **Ethics**.

In Part I, you will be able to find out something about your own values. You will be invited to think about exactly what some values are—friendship, for example—because we may not always know what we believe we know about values. Some values are shared by almost everyone. However, people often disagree about the meaning and importance of other values. What are *your* values and why do you think they are important?

> *"If we had hinges on our heads*
> *There wouldn't be no sin.*
> *'Cause we could take the bad stuff out*
> *And leave the good stuff in."*
> Shel Silverstein, poet and composer

Question #1—Plato

Are you a fair and just person?

"Please give it back to me."
"Why?
"Because you borrowed it and it's mine."

Have you ever been in this kind of situation? Imagine that you have borrowed a calculator from a friend. Now the friend wants you to return it. What is the just thing for you to do?

I. Read the four alternatives below, think about the situation, then write the letter representing your answer in the space provided:

A. Try to convince your friend that you still need it.
B. Keep it as long as you can; after all, you need a calculator.
C. Return it—the calculator is your friend's, not yours.
D. You can always make another friend; keep the calculator.

Write your answer here: _____

Remember, the question is "What is the just thing to do?"—not "What do I feel like doing in this situation?" If you chose A or B, then it seems that you think your own interests are more important than respecting your friend's interests or property. If you chose D, you value things more than friendship—or, at least, you value *this* thing more than keeping *this* friend.

Most people would choose C. The reason why is stated in C: The calculator is not yours. Therefore, even if you want to keep it for some reason, you ought to return it if the calculator—or anything you borrow—belongs to another person.

What does this example tell us about justice? In fact, just what is justice? This question is almost as old as philosophy itself. Philosophers have been asking this

DOI: 10.4324/9781003237150-3

question since the time of **Plato**, the famous Greek philosopher who lived from 427 to 347 B.C. However, the above example, which is taken from Book I of Plato's dialogue, the *Republic*, suggests that justice can be easily defined: It is treating other people fairly. In short, to be just is to be fair; so, whatever is borrowed should always be returned since that is what is fair in this case.

Is this a good definition? Let's change the example in a few ways (as Plato has Socrates do in the *Republic*). Imagine that an adult in your family borrows a weapon from a friend, and between the time that the weapon is borrowed and the time the friend wants it returned, the friend becomes mentally unstable. Now, according to the original definition, it would be just to return what has been borrowed—in this case, to return the weapon—since the definition says that whatever is borrowed should always be returned.

But, what do you think would be the just thing to do in this case?

II. Here are four alternatives. Place the letter for your answer in the space provided below:

> E. Keep the weapon; the friend is unstable, and what the friend will do with the weapon once it is returned is unknown.
> F. Return the weapon; after all, it's the friend's property.
> G. Talk to a philosopher and ask for the true definition of justice. Once you know this definition, then you will know what should be done.
> H. Try to get professional help for the friend.

Answer here: _____

Let's briefly look at the answers:

i. Answer (H) suggests that the friend is important. Although this attitude is good, it does not really help answer the question about the just thing to do in this instance. (Are you sure you know what it means to be a friend? See **Question #2.**)

ii. Answer (F) shows that you understand the original definition of justice and that you want to apply that definition. But, would it truly be just to return a weapon to someone if that individual were insane?

iii. Answer (E) eliminates the harmful consequences that might occur if an insane person had a weapon. However, to keep the weapon when it belongs to another person violates our definition of justice. Can a person act unjustly in order to do something good? Somehow this does not sound correct.

Did you select answer G? If you did, then one philosopher you could talk to is Socrates, Plato's teacher and the principal character in most of Plato's dialogues. The *Republic* analyzes the meaning of justice—but it is a lengthy attempt, about 300 pages! So, it seems safe to say that, whatever justice is, it will not be easily understood and described. Still, we can make a start in the direction that Plato thinks we should be heading.

"I think the first duty of society is justice."
Alexander Hamilton, statesman

For Further Thought

1. Should you be just to your enemies as well as to your friends?

2. Can you be unjust to yourself?

3. If the answer to 2 is yes, then can you also be *just* to yourself?

Plato thought that true justice begins in ourselves and that it is important to know ourselves as well as possible so that we can be just to ourselves whenever we speak, act, or make a choice. If we do know ourselves by thinking about who we are and what we want and how we hope to spend our lives, then it should be possible, eventually, to discover at least something about the nature of justice.

Keep this conclusion in mind as you do other questions in this book. When you ask yourself a question, especially a philosophical question, and then try to answer it, you are learning more about yourself. And, if Plato is right, you are also learning more about justice.

Of course, you are also being a philosopher.

Question #2—Aristotle

How do you know who your friends are?

The following statements may sound familiar:

"She's a friend of mine."
"Oh, he's my best friend!"
"You're not my friend anymore!"

We all have friends—or at least almost all of us do. It seems safe to say that a person who had no friends would not only be lonely, but also not very happy. Having friends seems to be an important part of being human, and it is also essential to leading a happy life. But, can we always tell who our friends are? To answer this question as a philosopher would, it is necessary to *define* the concept of friendship.

The Greek philosopher **Aristotle** (384–322 B.C.) thought this was a very important question. In the *Nicomachean Ethics* (named after Nicomacheas, one of Aristotle's sons), Aristotle spent much time and energy thinking about friendship. Let's see whether you agree with the way Aristotle defines friendship and with the types of friendship he describes.

The following are three descriptions of relationships between two people. In the space after each description, write "agree" or "disagree" to indicate whether you think the example is a type of friendship—"agree" if you think it is, "disagree" if you think it is not.

A. If John and Jim help each other with homework on a regular basis, are they friends? _____

B. If Mary and Liz like to do fun activities with one another, are they friends? _____

C. Pierre and Manuel frequently discuss important issues with one another. If they always try to help each other to do the right thing, are they friends? _____

DOI: 10.4324/9781003237150-4

If you answered "agree" to all three questions, then you are an Aristotelian, at least as far as friendship is concerned. For Aristotle, *all three* relationships are examples of friendship. Aristotle's definition of friendship includes three parts. All three parts must be present in a relationship in order for friendship to exist. Here is Aristotle's definition of friendship: Two people are friends with each other if

1. each person has good will toward the other person;
2. each person wishes good will toward the other person because of any one of the following three motives: usefulness, pleasure, or moral goodness. For Aristotle, acting toward another person from *any one* of these three motives is enough to produce a type of friendship; and,
3. each person *knows* that the other person has good will toward him or her. In other words, if Mary has good will toward Irene, but Irene does not know that Mary feels toward her in this way, then Mary and Irene are not friends.

For Aristotle, there are three types of friendship. Part 2 of Aristotle's definition shows that each type is based on one of the three motives that connect people with one another: usefulness, pleasure, or moral goodness. In the three examples given, Example A is a friendship based on usefulness, Example B is a friendship based on pleasure, Example C is a friendship based on moral goodness.

"A friend is one before whom I may think aloud."
Ralph Waldo Emerson, essayist and poet

For Further Thought

1. If you did not answer "agree" to all three examples, then ask yourself why you thought that one (or more) of the examples did *not* illustrate friendship. The following point might help you to clarify why you disagree with Aristotle.

2. One way philosophers test a definition is to try to think of a *counterexample* to that definition. A counterexample satisfies all the stated elements of the definition, but it describes a case that does not seem to fit the concept to be defined. Such a case is called a "counter"-example because, although the instance described is an example of the definition, it runs "counter" to the point of the definition. If you can think of a counterexample to a definition, then the definition is probably incomplete or perhaps even incorrect.

(Note: The discussion in **Question #1** contains a counterexample by Socrates showing that a definition of justice is inadequate.)

Here are two hints that might help you to state a counterexample to Aristotle's definition of friendship:

a. What does it mean to wish someone "good will"? For example, if you say "hi" to an acquaintance, are you wishing that person good will?

b. Can you make a friend in five minutes? How important is the element of time to forming a friendship?

3. Here is another way to evaluate Aristotle's definition of friendship. What percentage of your friendships are based on usefulness? On pleasure? On moral goodness?

4. If a friendship is based on either usefulness or pleasure, how long do you think this kind of friendship will last?

5. What is the difference between a friend and an acquaintance?

Question #3—Confucius

Should you be rewarded for your efforts in school?

Teachers and parents are always saying *"Do your best!"* and *"Try your hardest!"* But, should students be given credit for trying hard even if the results of their work are less than excellent?

Let's say that you are a middle school mathematics teacher. Your class is being graded according to the following scale:

A = 90–100
B = 80–89
C = 70–79
D = 60–69

All test scores, homework, projects, and so forth have been submitted to you. Here are the results of four students (identified by the numbers 1 through 4):

#1 tries very hard but scores 65%.
#2 exerts average effort and scores 76%.
#3 puts forth little effort but scores 86%.
#4 tries hardly at all but scores 89%.

As the teacher, you must assign grades to these students. What grade will you give them? Will you grade them only on the results of their work, or will you also include the effort that you saw them display throughout the term? Put the grade you select for each student in the spaces below:

Student 1   Student 2   Student 3   Student 4

Grade: _____   Grade: _____   Grade: _____   Grade: _____

DOI: 10.4324/9781003237150-5

There are a number of possibilities, but if you gave some (or all) of the students credit for their effort so that their final grade is higher than the scores justified on the grading scale, then you would disagree with the Chinese philosopher **Confucius** (551–479 B.C.). And, even if you were strict and graded the students only on results, ignoring effort altogether, you will still be interested in the issues that emerge from what Confucius says.

Confucius' ideas are expressed in *aphorisms*. An aphorism is a short statement that intends to say something true. In one aphorism, Confucius says that the more effort people must exert in order to learn, the less valuable these people are. In short, it's results that count, not effort.

What Confucius is saying might seem harsh, but keep in mind that he lived long ago and in a culture very different from the one in which most of us are living. As a result, some of these differences might affect how he viewed, and thought about, his world. Also, Confucius was very practical. He thought that if someone had to work hard—or, indeed, very hard—in order to learn, then that person probably did not have much natural intelligence. Therefore, over time, this person probably could not learn very much and, as a result, would not be as useful to society as someone who could learn very quickly. In this aphorism, Confucius emphasizes the value of natural intelligence and the practical benefits that result from using one's intelligence. Effort is certainly important, of course, and everyone should be encouraged to try their best. The question is whether effort should be rewarded in the same way as results.

For Further Thought

1. One way to evaluate or assess a philosopher's ideas is to try to identify what the philosopher is assuming. All philosophers make *assumptions*. It is often important to realize what a philosopher has assumed before you evaluate what he or she has thought about some problem or question. What do you think Confucius is assuming about intelligence and also about the relation between effort and intelligence?

   Here are some questions that may help you to identify Confucius' assumptions:

   A. Does intelligence vary from person to person?
   B. Does one person's intelligence vary from subject to subject?
   C. Can intelligence increase, or does it remain the same?

2. Think about your answers to questions A, B, and C. Then ask yourself: Why should effort be rewarded? The answers provided for questions A, B, and C should offer hints for answering this question.

    Note: If it is true that effort should be rewarded, then the aphorism we have been examining would not seem to be correct; or, at least, it should be modified. But, keep in mind that the philosophy of Confucius is complex and subtle, and what he says in other aphorisms about intelligence, effort, and a person's place in society may be relevant to what he was saying in this one. So, even if we disagree with Confucius here, it is important to do our best to understand his overall position and the reasons he would give to back up his point.

3. For discussion of another issue in which identifying a philosopher's assumptions is very important, see **Question #5**.

"Success is counted sweetest
By those who ne'er succeed."
Emily Dickinson, poet

Question #4—Marcus Aurelius

Should you let little things bother you?

Well . . . why not? Even though they are little things, if they bother you, then they bother you! Who's to say what should and should not bother a person? But, this question is not as simple as it might appear at first glance, at least if we think about it philosophically.

Marcus Aurelius (121–180 A.D.) was Emperor of Rome from 160 to 180 A.D. According to historians, he was one of the most just of the Roman Emperors in administering to the needs of the Empire. When Marcus Aurelius was in battle, leading the Roman legions against invaders, he would frequently sit in his tent at night and reflect on the day's events and what they meant to him. His thoughts were eventually published under the title of *Meditations*, and they stand today as one of the most important contributions to the type of ethical philosophy known as *stoicism*.

Are you a "stoic"? You can determine whether or not you are by answering the following set of questions either "yes" or "no" in the space provided. Try to answer as honestly as you can. You will see that little things can perhaps mean a lot depending on how we react to them.

1. Can you study even with a bit of a headache? _____
2. If your classroom is too cool or too warm, can you still concentrate on the day's lessons? _____
3. If you get hungry in mid-afternoon, can you still concentrate on schoolwork or other activities? _____
4. Is it okay if your trip to school happens in the rain? _____
5. If you honestly believe you did a thorough job studying for a test, but the test includes questions on points for which you did not prepare, can you take it in stride and not become upset? _____
6. If someone at school likes to tease you now and then, can you ignore it and not want to "get back" at this person? _____
7. If your favorite sports team loses a close game, do you get over your disappointment quickly? _____

DOI: 10.4324/9781003237150-6

If you answered "yes" to all seven questions, then you are immediately eligible for membership in the *Club of Stoics*! Marcus Aurelius would say that you have recognized that some things in life that might seem to be important are not really important, and that knowing this fact is essential. On the other hand, the more "no" answers you have, the less you should consider yourself to be a stoical person. In the end, it is up to you to decide whether or not the way a stoic reacts to the world is the type of person you want to be.

Marcus Aurelius would add that, in order to be a good stoic, it is not enough just to ignore little things. It is also very important to learn as much as possible about what you ought to do and then try your very best to do it. So, being a stoic means not just ignoring little things, but also finding out about "big things"—in other words, your duty—and then doing these big things as best you can.

For Further Thought

1. At one point in the *Meditations*, Marcus Aurelius summarizes his position in a very few words: "*I do my duty; other things trouble me not.*" You have a number of duties—to your parents, your teachers, your friends, and also to yourself. List some of these duties in the spaces below:

   Duties to Parents: _____
   _____

   Duties to Teachers: _____
   _____

   Duties to Friends: _____
   _____

   Duties to Yourself: _____
   _____

2. What is more important, doing your duty or trying to be happy? (See **Question #6** for a discussion of the concept of happiness.)

> *"I slept, and dreamed that life was Beauty;*
> *I woke, and found that life was Duty."*
> Ellen Sturgis Hooper, poet

Question #5—Moses Maimonides

Is it your duty to give to charity?

For Marcus Aurelius (**Question #4**), doing our duty is the most important value. But, do we have a duty to give to charity? Or, should giving to charity be only a matter of personal choice? If so, then one person can decide to be charitable and another person can decide not to be charitable, and both decisions are correct.

Moses Maimonides (1135–1204) was one of the most important philosophers of the medieval period and is also considered to be one of the most important Jewish philosophers of all time. Maimonides thought that giving to charity was a duty. Of course, we could decide not to give to charity, but for Maimonides we would not be doing our duty if we made this decision.

Let's see what your attitude is toward giving to charity. Answer the following questions "yes" or "no," depending on what you think. Try to be as honest as possible in giving your answers.

1. If you were very wealthy, would you give some of your money to charity? _____
2. If you made a comfortable living, but were not wealthy, would you give some of your money to charity? _____
3. If you see a homeless person asking for charity and you happened to have some extra money with you, would you give it to that person? _____
4. If you give money to a homeless person, would you do so not just to avoid feeling guilty, but because it is the right thing to do? _____
5. When you read or hear about people who are starving in various parts of the world (including the United States), do you usually think about whether something should be done to help these people? _____

questions continued on the next page

DOI: 10.4324/9781003237150-7

6. If you believe in God and God says (through Scripture) that the poor must be helped through charity, would these reasons convince you that you have a duty to give to charity? _____

7. If you were an adult and working for your living, would you be willing to donate a small part of your income so that society could prevent poverty altogether by providing educations, homes, and jobs for everyone? _____

If you answered "yes" to questions 1–5, then from Maimonides' perspective you are a morally virtuous person regarding charity. Each "no" answer for questions 1–5 tends to decrease the degree to which you are virtuous about charity, again according to Maimonides. And, if you answered "no" for all questions 1–5, then Maimonides would invite you, first, to ask yourself whether you might be somewhat too self-centered and, second, to wonder about the effect of this attitude on your own moral character.

Now, review your answer to question 6. If your answer is "yes," then you would agree with Maimonides' reason for claiming that charity is a duty. For Maimonides, since Scripture says that we must be charitable and since Scripture comes ultimately from God, then charity is a duty for the simple reason that God *says* that it is a duty. And surely it is a duty for us to do what God tells us to do.

For Further Thought

1. Maimonides' position is philosophically strong, but only if two very important assumptions are granted. And it is true that either or both of these assumptions have been denied by thoughtful people. Look again at question 6 and think about what it is asking. Then, see whether you can identify the two assumptions that are part of the content of question 6.

Assumption One:

Assumption Two:

2. Now consider question 7 and ask yourself, Which groups of people are better off in a society where the need for charity has been completely eliminated? If you answered "yes" to question 7, then you should be able to answer this question. (Hint: What is question 7 asking you to do?) Even if you

answered "no" to 7, you should be able to take the hint just offered and answer the question about who is better off in a society where charity has been eliminated.

Here is one way to consider this problem: Charity is necessary when poverty is present in a society. Therefore, if there is no poverty, then there is no need for charity. Who then would be better off in such a society? Answer: *Everyone*! First, poor people would no longer be poor; second, all the people with adequate incomes would not have to support the poor through their taxes or through donations to charity. So, if everyone in a society would be better off if poverty could be eliminated, should everyone in that society contribute some of their income to prevent poverty? Would it be their *duty* to do so?

This is a question about the importance of values that the members of the society would have to decide for themselves. What do you think?

"In faith and hope the world will disagree,
But all mankind's concern is charity."
Alexander Pope, poet

Question #6—John Stuart Mill

Will having fun make you happier than studying?

"I had a pleasant time with my mind, for it was happy."
Louisa May Alcott, novelist

Perhaps you would not hesitate to answer this question with a loud "Yes!," thinking of whatever it is that you really enjoy doing. After all, how many people truly like to study? But a philosopher would hesitate, at least for a bit, when this question is asked. Why? Because from a philosophical perspective, the answer to the question depends on the meaning of the concept of "happiness." The activity below will give you a chance to think about happiness in ways that might be new and interesting.

The following list represents *eight* types of activities. Assume that *all eight* of these activities will be included in a "happy" life. Review the eight and rank them from 1 to 8 according to how important you think they are as far as being elements in happiness. Thus, a ranking of 8 means "least important," 1 means "most important," and the other six activities should be ranked in order between those two extremes.

Probably everyone would put sitting in a dentist's chair as #8, the least important activity in a happy life. The reason is obvious: Going to the dentist usually means experiencing some discomfort. But, think about why you go to the dentist, and you'll get an insight into the meaning of happiness. And, as you rank the other activities, you will begin to appreciate why the concept of happiness is very difficult for philosophers to define.

This activity is even more interesting if you do it with other people, friends, or classmates. Make a copy of these pages, enough for everyone who wants to participate. Then have each person rank the activities. When everyone is finished, compare your rankings.

24

DOI: 10.4324/9781003237150-8

a. Sitting in a dentist's chair. _____

b. Eating your favorite food. _____

c. Playing a game. _____

d. Reading a book. _____

e Sitting deep in thought with other students. _____

f. Having fun with a friend. _____

g. Helping a classmate with homework. _____

h. Discussing an interesting topic. _____

How high did you rate d, e, g, and h? In fact, would you agree that these activities should be considered as elements in happiness in the first place?

According to **John Stuart Mill** (1806–1873), happiness can be defined as the greatest degree of pleasure for the greatest number of people. Mill called this principle **utilitarianism**. However, happiness understood as the *greatest* degree of pleasure also includes the *least* amount of pain. In addition, Mill insisted that not all pleasures were identical in value and that some pleasures were more desirable than others (e.g., the pleasures of learning and conversation).

So, in order to be happy—and a good utilitarian—you should do things you enjoy, *as well as* study, since studying will prepare you to lead a way of life that will realize your potential as fully as possible. It may not always be "fun" to study, but if Mill is correct, then happiness and having fun are not the same! Also, you should act in your own best interests, but you should do so by taking into account the best interests of other people as well. Remember that *everyone* wants to be happy; as a result, if people help other people, then that increases the total amount of happiness.

For Further Thought

1. Is happiness a feeling you have or a state you are in? In other words, can you *be* happy without necessarily *feeling* happy? If happiness is a feeling, then it will come and go; but, if happiness is a state, then it might be much more permanent. Is happiness for Mill a feeling or a state (or, perhaps, a combination of both)?

2. Happiness includes feeling content about your life *and* doing good things for others. Do you agree or disagree?

3. Compare your rankings of the eight activities with that of a friend or with classmates. If your rankings differ, see whether their reasons for ranking the

activities in a different order might make you reconsider why you ranked the activities as you did.

"A great obstacle to happiness is to expect too much happiness."
Bernard Fontenelle, author

Question #7—Immanuel Kant

Should you ever tell a lie?

What is a lie? A simple definition is that a lie occurs whenever you tell someone that something is true when you know it is *not* true. We often hear that it is wrong to tell a lie. But, is it *always* wrong to tell a lie? Should we *always* try to tell the truth? These are serious questions. They are serious because we believe that the truth is very important, and that it is important to protect the truth. But, is it *always* important to tell the truth?

Read the following circumstances where telling a lie is a possible course of action. Think about the circumstances, and in each case answer—as honestly as possible—whether you would tell a lie. If you would tell a lie, answer "yes." If you would not tell a lie, answer "no."

1. If your mother asks whether you had a cookie before dinner (you did indeed have that cookie), would you lie and deny it? _____

2. If your best friend is wearing an extremely unattractive outfit, would you tell her she looks great even though you honestly think that she looks like a walking disaster? _____

3. If you knew you could get someone you really don't like into trouble by telling a lie about that person, would you do it? _____

4. If you knew you could get accepted at a very good university by lying on your application for admission, would you do it? _____

5. If you could become wealthy by telling a lie, would you do it? _____

6. If you could save a person's life by telling a lie, would you do it? _____

DOI: 10.4324/9781003237150-9

Did you answer "yes" to any of the six examples? If so, then you would disagree with the important German philosopher **Immanuel Kant** (1724–1804) about whether or not telling a lie is ever justified.

Whenever we lie, we are damaging the truth. And for Kant, we are also damaging ourselves if we lie. Kant believed that it was essential that we do the right thing for the right reason. Since lying is intentionally falsifying the truth, lying is wrong.

Kant argued that if we lie because of certain circumstances, then we would be trying to twist a wrong action into a correct one. But, to attempt this is to throw our minds and moral natures into confusion. Kant thought that trying to achieve what seems to be a *good* result by using a *bad* means is irrational—it is a contradiction. So, if our nature is to be rational, then a lie is wrong—and always wrong—because to tell a lie would be to go against our nature as rational. Therefore, we would be harming ourselves as human beings even if our intention was to help others.

For Kant, rationality is part of what all human beings share. Kant thought that it was more important to preserve our nature as rational than to lie in order to achieve a certain result, even if that result seems good. So, for Kant, the *end* (e.g., saving a person's life) does not justify the *means* (telling a lie in order to achieve that end). Under no circumstances are we to sacrifice our nature as rational beings in order to achieve a certain end.

For Further Thought

1. You may have noticed a pattern in the series of examples given in the activity. They were in an ascending scale of seriousness, from relatively trivial or harmless to a situation involving life and death. Also, some of the examples involved only you, some involved other people. How would you justify—philosophically—telling a lie if you thought you would do so in any one (or more than one) of the situations described in those examples?

2. One way to justify a lie would be to consider the related concepts of means and ends. Is it possible to argue *against* Kant's understanding of the relation between means and ends in the context of telling a lie? In other words, can you think of circumstances in which telling a lie would be justified?

3. Do you think you could ever lie to yourself? See **Question #18** for discussion of this fascinating question.

"Lying is an indispensable part of making life tolerable."
Bergen Evans, writer and humorist

28

Question #8—Martin Luther King, Jr.

Are there times when you should be violent?

Have you ever been really angry at someone? So angry that you wanted to hit the person or do something violent to that person?

Such anger is not unusual; the problem is knowing what to do with this kind of intense emotion so that nothing happens that we will regret later. On other occasions and in different circumstances, groups of people have used violence in order to achieve their goals. Thus, when one nation tries to conquer another nation through warfare, that is the same kind of tactic—armed violence. People throughout history have always sought to achieve their ends in this way. But just because many people have acted in this way, does that fact make this approach right (see **Question #36**)? Are they ethically correct to do so?

Carefully consider the situations described in each of the following three statements. Then, indicate whether you agree with the point of the statement by writing "true" or "false" in the space provided:

1. If you have been continually harassed and bothered by the class bully, you are justified in retaliating by hitting this person. _____

2. If you belong to a group of people who, for some reason, have been treated unjustly, you and your group are justified in using violence in order to seek justice. _____

3. If your country has been attacked by another country, you are justified in using violence in order to protect your country. _____

Martin Luther King, Jr. (1929–1968) is not usually considered a philosopher, not in the way that Plato or Kant would be. However, in his speeches and

DOI: 10.4324/9781003237150-10

writings, he argued just as a philosopher would: by presenting definitions, drawing distinctions, and reasoning to conclusions.

King followed and developed the thought of the Indian leader **Mohandas Gandhi** (1869–1948), who taught that the best way to achieve social justice was through nonviolent means. King's argument is, simply put, that the end does not justify the means. If violence had to be used in order to achieve social justice for oppressed peoples, then, for King, attaining social justice in this way is immoral. King believed that all human beings are made in the image of God; therefore, to strike or harm another human being is, in a sense, to strike at God. The most effective way to achieve social justice is to use nonviolent means in order to show the world how seriously the oppressed people wanted their end. These people wanted it with such passion and intensity that they were willing to suffer, go to jail, even die for the rightness of their cause.

King would argue that there are more effective—and morally correct—ways to deal with bullies, oppression, and personal attack. Do you agree?

"Answer violence with violence!"
Juan Perón, political leader

For Further Thought

1. Ask some of your friends or classmates whether they think that there are times when a person should be violent. If they answer "yes," make a list of the examples they give that justify the use of violence. Then, discuss these examples with them, using Martin Luther King, Jr.'s principles of nonviolence.

2. Is nonviolence the best way to achieve social justice in the world? As you reflect on this question, think about what Martin Luther King, Jr. accomplished by his teachings and by the example of his life.

3. Mohandas Gandhi and Martin Luther King, Jr., influential advocates of nonviolence, were both assassinated. It is one of the tragic ironies of history that these two champions of peace and universal brotherhood died as they did. There are times when saying what you believe is true, which is what philosophers try to do, requires tremendous courage.

Question #9—Simone de Beauvoir

Do you sometimes feel weird when you are with others?

Humanity is "one undivided and indivisible family . . . ."
Mohandas Gandhi, spiritual leader

Who doesn't? This awkward sensation seems to be part of our nature as human beings. But, have you ever wondered what the reason might be for this reaction?

The following is a personal inventory list that will help measure what we'll call your social "comfort zone." Ten situations are sketched. You probably have not been personally involved in all 10; skip the ones that do not apply. For the situations in which you have personal experience, think about what it was like to be involved in them—and be honest with yourself and your feelings. Then, in the space provided, give a numerical measure for your comfort zone according to the following scale of feelings:

Nice and relaxed.	1 pt.
A bit on the tense side.	2 pts.
Nervous but bearable.	3 pts.
Get me out of here!	4 pts.

(You might also ask friends or classmates whether they want to take the comfort zone evaluation.)

A. At home with your family.   _____
B. With friends at a shopping mall.   _____
C. At a party where you don't know many people.   _____
D. In a group where everyone is of the opposite sex. _____

questions continued on the next page

DOI: 10.4324/9781003237150-11

E. In a racially mixed group.   _____
F. In a group where everyone is a different race than you.   _____
G. Your first day at a new school.   _____
H. Moving to a new city.   _____
I. Visiting a new country.   _____
J. Moving to a new country.   _____

Total   _____

Determine your total number of points. The closer your score is to 10, the more comfortable you are in a wide variety of circumstances. However, the more your total approaches 40, the more you can appreciate the influence of what the philosopher **Simone de Beauvoir** (1908–1986) calls "the Other."

What is common to all 10 situations listed above? All of them are social situations of one sort or another. All involve *people*. At one very basic level, all people are the same. They have bodies, minds, feelings, attitudes, likes, dislikes, fears, hopes, and so forth. But, at another level, many differences exist between and among people: cultural and ethnic background, physical appearance, intellectual ability, talent, preferences, individual style, and so forth.

In the 10 situations listed above, *you* are an example of "the Other," or of being an outsider. The degree to which you feel awkward or "out of place" depends on the fact that you are, in some way, "other" than the rest of the people who are present in that situation.

Simone de Beauvoir discusses "the Other" in *The Second Sex*. Her main concern in this work is the "otherness"—or a feeling of being somehow apart—that exists between men and women. But, she also affirms that otherness occurs throughout the human race: It is found not only in gender, but also between nations, races, cultures, and age groups.

Philosophers since the early Greeks have been interested in studying the *social nature* of human beings, in contrast to what human beings do and achieve as individuals. Madame de Beauvoir's development of the concept of "the Other" provides a dramatic and useful entry into thinking about how we relate to people and how in many situations—too many—these relations could be improved.

For Further Thought

1. If you gave a 3 or 4 for any of the situations listed, ask yourself why your comfort level is so low. Can you identify the factors that contribute to your more intense feeling of "otherness" in these situations?

2. Compare your comfort zone with those of your friends and classmates. There will be differences, of course, since different people will react in different ways when they are with other people. But, it will be interesting and informative to discuss these differences when two people have different ratings for the same situation.

   For example, if you are generally relaxed with people of other races but a friend or classmate finds these situations to be awkward and tense, you could try to explain why you do not feel "other" than those individuals. This kind of discussion may help to break down barriers that keep people from interacting with certain "other" people precisely because the barriers are hidden. The more we increase our awareness of the otherness of people and why this otherness is strong, the less "other" these people will become.

"One of the greatest necessities in America
is to discover creative solitude."
Carl Sandburg, poet

Question #10—Martin Heidegger

Do we control technology, or does technology control us?

Our word *technology* comes from a Greek word that means "art" or "craft." So, in a sense, technology is almost everywhere we look, since we are surrounded by things produced by art or craft. If at night we enjoy looking at the stars, but we have to do so through glasses to correct nearsightedness, then our enjoyment of something purely natural includes a technological factor. In general, it seems that anything human beings do that is *not* natural involves us in some way with technology.

Below are a series of observations about technology in the world today. In the space provided, indicate whether you think that each observation is "true" or "false."

1. Automobiles will eventually be made so that they will not cause excessive harm to the environment. _____
2. Agriculture specialists will determine ways to feed the world's growing population and eliminate hunger. _____
3. Human beings can stop doing research on computer technology whenever they decide it is to their advantage to do so. _____
4. Global warming is not a serious problem. _____
5. The needs of technology will never consume natural resources to the point of causing serious harm to future human beings. _____
6. The advantages of technology outweigh the disadvantages. _____
7. Modern human beings do not rely too much on technology. _____
8. Life is better now than 100 years ago because of technology. _____
9. Technology is nothing more than a means to an end. _____

34

DOI: 10.4324/9781003237150-12

If you answered "true" to all nine statements, then you have no concerns about technology. However, the more "false" answers you gave, the more you believe that technology presents a problem to us. And, if you put "false" to question 9, you agree with an important 20th-century philosopher, **Martin Heidegger** (1889–1976). Heidegger thought that technology is *not* just a means to an end. For Heidegger, our need to interact with nature by controlling it for our purposes shows something about who we are as human beings. In other words, the "means to an end" way of approaching the significance of technology is far too simple.

Heidegger believed that it is essential that we think about what we are doing and why we are doing it in order to understand fully the meaning behind technology. When we take something from a natural source and then transform it into a thing for purposes of improving human life, Heidegger thought that we are showing something very important about our relation to nature, to that part of reality that is "other" than human beings (see **Question #9**).

Do we control technology or does technology control us? If Heidegger's approach to this question is correct, then the answer is not as simple as it might seem. It is one of the most important questions currently facing us and our relation to the natural world. Will we know what to do if technology threatens to move beyond our control? The answer to this question assumes that we understand what it means to know something, in this case, technology. Do we have this kind of understanding?

For Further Thought

1. Take a look around your home or school. Notice how many things are technological. Think about whether each of these things has advantages. Then ask yourself whether they also have disadvantages: Are they in some way harmful to our lives as human beings or to the environment?

2. Let's apply the results of your investigations to Question 1: List three examples of technology that you believe are the most useful and important to human happiness. Why are they useful? Now, list three examples of technology that you believe are the most harmful to the environment or to the quality of our life. Why are they harmful?

"Lo! Men have become the tools of their tools."
Henry David Thoreau, author

PART II

Knowledge

What do you know? Many things, of course. But have you ever wondered about *how* you know what you know? If you look at a stick placed in water, the stick looks bent. But is it really bent? If not, how do you know that it is not bent? Also, what then *are* you looking at when you do see a bent stick in the water? If on a hot, sunny day you see a mirage in the distance, what sort of thing are you seeing? Philosophers have wondered about these kinds of questions, and long ago they discovered that the process of knowing is complex—but also extremely fascinating.

In this section, you will be challenged by—and enjoy—some of the questions in the branch of philosophy called **Epistemology**. Epistemology is the inquiry concerned with explaining how we know. Exploring the questions in this section might not make you any smarter than you already are, but they will help explain why you know as much as you do!

"Knowledge is the antidote to fear."
Ralph Waldo Emerson, essayist and poet

Question #11—Zeno

How do you know for certain that things move?

"There is nothing permanent except change."
Heraclitus, Greek philosopher

"Who's faster?"
"I am, that's obvious."
"No, I am!"
"I know, let's race!"

Most of us have been in a race. Perhaps you have won a race or two, perhaps not—for present purposes, it doesn't matter. What now concerns us is much more basic than who wins a race. The question is: Do races ever really happen in the first place?

Answer these questions "true" or "false" in the spaces provided:

1. Some things are in motion. _____
2. How I know that some things are in motion
    is easy to explain. _____

It would be very difficult not to put "true" for question 1. It would probably also be very difficult not to put "true" for question 2. But, how do you know that things move? The answer seems obvious: because you *see* them move! What could possibly be interesting or important about something so simple and evident?

Philosophers are very skilled at recognizing the mystery in everyday experiences and occurrences, things that seem so common and ordinary that we take them for granted as "obvious."

DOI: 10.4324/9781003237150-13

The early Greek philosopher Parmenides (c.515–440 B.C.) was such a thinker. Parmenides had a student named **Zeno** (c.495–430 B.C.), who believed in Parmenides' ideas—and tried to prove them. Zeno did this in a very interesting way: by constructing paradoxes. A **paradox** is like a contradiction that cannot be explained. In this case, Zeno tried to show that motion was only an illusion. Although it certainly appears as if things move, when we think about motion and try to explain what motion is we discover that the way things look can be very deceiving.

Here is one of Zeno's most famous paradoxes: Imagine the great Greek hero and athlete Achilles being challenged to a race—by an extremely poky Tortoise! Obviously, Achilles has a huge advantage, so let's make the race a bit more fair by giving the Tortoise a head start. Both contestants, Achilles and the Tortoise, are at the starting line, but the Tortoise (T) starts at a point ahead of Achilles (A):

T _____

A _____

They're off!! The Tortoise lumbers along
while Achilles zooms ahead. Until . . .

T _____

A _____xxxxxxxxxxxxx

Achilles reaches the exact point where the Tortoise started the race.
But, in the meantime, the Tortoise has crept a bit further along. So . . .

T _____yyyy

A _____xxxxxxxxxxxx

Achilles is beginning to sweat. He reaches the exact point where
Tortoise was . . . but, again, during that brief interval the Tortoise
has crept just a bit further ahead. And so . . .

T_____zz

A_____xxxxxxxxxxxxyyyy

F
I
N
I
S
H

L
I
N
E

Can you see what will happen and, according to Zeno, what will continue to happen during this strange race? Not only will Achilles not win the race, not only will Achilles not pass the Tortoise, Achilles will never even reach a point *equal to* where the Tortoise is. Why? Because the Tortoise, moving all the time, will continue to edge ahead just a tiny, tiny bit during the time it takes Achilles to reach the point where the Tortoise previously was. If you bet on Achilles to win this race, sorry—you lose! Why? For the simple reason that a race requires motion and motion, when we try to understand it as explained above, becomes impossible. We may *believe* we see motion happening in this race, but Zeno has shown that if we *think* about what we see, we realize that our eyes are playing paradoxical tricks on us. In fact, the race never really got started—it just looked like it did!

What's going on here? You and Zeno are looking at exactly the same race. Zeno has offered his explanation of that race. You know that you are right—Achilles will easily win the race—and you also know that Zeno is wrong. But, Zeno has explained his position in a philosophical way; therefore, to prove philosophically that Zeno is wrong, you must also explain your position by showing how Zeno's explanation has gone wrong.

Zeno's explanation of the race between Achilles and the Tortoise is a fascinating paradox. One reason the paradox is so fascinating is because it seems so simple to show—or to try to show—how we know that things move. But, if Zeno is correct, then we cannot explain how we know that things move for a very simple reason—things do not really move! It just *looks* like they do.

For Further Thought

1. The philosopher Aristotle (see **Questions #2** and **#12**) said this about motion: "*Motion is easy to see but hard to understand.*" Think about motion: Do you know that something moves because you see it move, or do you know about motion because of some other reason?

2. Do you know about things that happen in the world in ways other than through sight or hearing or touch or taste or smell?

3. How do you know about the numbers you use when you do mathematics—through sight or in some other way? (For more discussion of numbers as mysterious and philosophically interesting, see **Question #23**).

4. How we explain what happens when things move is fascinating and not easily done. In fact, explaining how we *know* anything is even more challenging. (See **Question #16** for discussion of this issue.)

5. For a very different kind of paradox than the type Zeno created (and at least as intriguing!), see **Question #38**.

"It requires a very unusual mind to make an analysis of the obvious."
Alfred North Whitehead, mathematician and philosopher

Question #12—Aristotle

What makes something you say true?

"Mental activity is easy if it doesn't have to conform to reality."
Marcel Proust, novelist

As a rule, we want to say things that are true—at least most of the time. Sometimes, it might seem useful—especially when we are in some sort of trouble—to tell a lie (but see **Question #7**) in order to remove ourselves from this difficulty, whatever it may be. Normally, however, we place a high value on truth and we try to establish it and, once it has been established, we try to preserve the truth as true.

But, determining just what is true and why it is true is not an easy thing to do. Philosophers since the ancient Greeks have been wondering about, and thinking about, the question of the nature of truth.

Imagine that you are in school. You are taking an examination. It is a "true/false" test, a type of test most students experience fairly often. But did you ever wonder what it meant to indicate that a given statement was "true" rather than "false"?

Here is a true/false examination that will lead you toward one philosopher's theory of truth. Put an X next to the answer that you think is correct:

1. If many people believe that something is true, then that something must be true.   T ____ F ____
2. If you say something and I believe it, then whatever you said is true.   T ____ F ____
3. If I say something and I believe that what I say is true, then it is true.   T ____ F ____

questions continued on the next page

DOI: 10.4324/9781003237150-14

4. If you say something and you believe that it is true,
   and if I say just the opposite and I believe that
   it is true, then we have both said something true.   T _____ F _____

5. If you say something and whatever you say
   corresponds to the way things are, then whatever
   you have said is true—even if I think and say
   just the opposite.   T _____ F _____

In the *Categories*, one of his works on *logic*, the Greek philosopher **Aristotle** (384–322 B.C.) says that *"it is by the facts of the case, by their being or not being so, that a statement is called true or false."* This is called the *Correspondence Theory of Truth*. The theory says, first, that only propositions can be true or false and, second, that *Propositions*—sentences that assert or deny something—are true when they "correspond" to facts, to the way things are in the world. So if you followed Aristotle's theory, then you would have answered the first four of the above questions "false" and only the fifth question "true."

Let's now consider a very easy true/false question:

The earth is round.   T _____ F _____

Naturally you checked "true." Why? Because it is true that the earth is round (or, more accurately, spherical). But, how do you know that it is round? Because it is an observable fact. Thus, the proposition "The earth is round" is true because it corresponds to the way things are.

For Further Thought

If Aristotle's theory of truth is correct, can you see why the answers to the first four questions above must be "false"? Let's quickly examine the answers:

1. If everyone believes that the earth is flat—as almost everyone did for centuries—does that belief make the earth flat? Of course not! The earth was, is, and remains round even when everyone thought it was flat (see **Question #36**).

2. If I believe you when you say something, does that belief make whatever you say true? No. You could be wrong and I might not know any better. In this case, we are *both* wrong.

3. If I say something and believe that it is true, does that make it true? No. I am simply mistaken in my belief. How often do these kind of mistakes happen? Often! This is why it is so important to know as much as we can about the way things are in the world.

4. Can two opposed propositions both be true? No. One is wrong, and perhaps both are wrong! For example, if you believe that "All apples are red," and I believe that "No apples are red," then both of us are mistaken since it is true that only some apples are red. The problem is whether you or your friend (or both!) is saying something false—even though you (or your friend) might believe it is true.

"Hard are the ways of truth, and rough to walk."
John Milton, poet

Question #13—René Descartes

Can you doubt that you exist?

This seems to be an odd thing to ask, but thinking about this question will lead you directly into one of the most important areas in epistemology, the question of determining the nature of *certitude*. The questions below represent a series of thoughts from the *Meditations on First Philosophy* by the important French philosopher **René Descartes** (1596–1650).

Descartes (pronounced "Day-cart") wanted to establish absolute certainty as the foundation for stating philosophical truths. In order to discover this certainty—if there was such a thing—he intentionally doubted everything it was possible to doubt. (Descartes called this procedure "methodic doubt.") Descartes reasoned that if he could locate something that could *never* be doubted, then he would be in contact with something that was necessary and absolutely certain. So, for Descartes, "possible" means "can be doubted." In other words, if something is only possible, then that something is capable of being doubted.

Remember that, if there is any way at all something *can* be doubted, then according to Descartes it *must* be doubted. What we want to discover, if we can, is something that can *never, ever* be doubted.

Let us follow Descartes as he doubts. Keep in mind that, if there is any way at all something can be doubted, then it cannot be the source of certitude. With that condition in mind—and after thinking carefully—answer the following questions "true" or "false:"

1. It is possible that the wall I am looking at does not really exist.   T _____ F _____
2. It is possible that I do not really have a body.   T _____ F _____
3. It is possible that I am dreaming right now.   T _____ F _____
4. It is possible that 3 + 2 does not equal 5.   T _____ F _____

DOI: 10.4324/9781003237150-15

45

If you answered "true" to all four of the above questions, then you are a good Cartesian, that is, a follower of Descartes! But, if you answered "false" to any *one* (or more) of the four questions, then Descartes would ask you to think just a bit harder. If you do, you will realize that circumstances can indeed exist in which what you thought was certain might not really be so.

For example, could there be an "evil demon," less powerful than God but more powerful than human beings, who confuses all of us about things such as 3 + 2 = 5, making us think that 3 + 2 = 5 when it really does not? Descartes says yes, it is possible that such a being could exist. If so, then *all four* of the possibilities mentioned above could be true.

Now for the Cartesian *coup de grace*—the answer to this question will throw you squarely into Descartes' philosophical lap! Answer the following question "true" or "false."

5. It is possible to doubt that you exist.   T _____ F _____

Can you doubt that you exist! No—or, as the French might say, "*Non Monsieur!*" Just think—if you *are* doubting that you exist, then you must be *existing* in order to doubt! One cannot doubt unless one exists, *eh bien*? So if it is false that it is possible to doubt that you exist, then you necessarily exist every time you doubt something, or every time that you think about something.

Voila! Descartes has found it! He has discovered the source of certitude—it is the self, or as he calls it, the "thinking thing." The point may be summarized thus: "I think, therefore I am" (or, to use the well-known Latin phrase, *cogito ergo sum*). From this starting point, Descartes begins to reason about himself and everything other than himself, including God, the sciences, and mathematics. Descartes' thinking was so important and so fertile for philosophers who came afterward—even the philosophers who disagreed with him—that Descartes is frequently referred to as "the father of modern philosophy."

For Further Thought

1. Descartes' position on thinking as the source of certitude is important for the way we understand the mind. For example, is the mind the same as the brain? Many contemporary scientists who study the brain answer this question "yes." What we call the mind is simply, and more accurately, various regions in the brain, each performing a certain "mental" function.

2. If Descartes were asked whether the mind is identical to the brain, what do you think he would say? Perhaps you could apply Descartes' method of doubt to determine the answer he would give.

3. Here is another way to approach the question "Is the mind identical to the brain?" If a material thing can be divided into parts, then Descartes calls this the property of being "divisible." On the other hand, he argues that the mind is "indivisible," that is, the mind cannot be broken into parts. In the 6th Meditation of the *Meditations on First Philosophy*, he gives a number of reasons to support this conclusion, one of which is that when I think of myself sensing, or imagining, doubting, or wishing, it is one and the same "me" doing all these activities. For Descartes, this fact is evidence that the mind is indivisible, that is, it cannot be broken into parts.

   Which position do you think makes more sense: the contemporary scientific view that maintains that the mind is the same as the brain, or the Cartesian position that maintains that the mind and the brain are not identical to one another? This is a fascinating—and difficult—question.

"Certainty generally is illusion . . . ."
Oliver Wendell Holmes, jurist

Question #14—George ("Bishop") Berkeley

Does a tree make a sound if it falls in a forest with no one around?

This is a philosophical "chestnut," that is, a question that has been around for a long time. It is also a question that can produce heated discussion since there seem to be good reasons for answering it either way—yes, the tree will make a sound; no, the tree will not make a sound.

These two answers—yes or no—seem to be the only two possible answers to the question as it is stated above. And yet . . . Let's try an unusual experiment. Imagine that you are in an auditorium, perhaps that of your school (the location does not matter). You are reciting a story to a packed house. This is the story you recite:

Once upon a time there were two young philosophers. They were walking in the woods, enjoying the sounds and sights of a beautiful spring day. The birds were singing, the leaves were gently rustling from the soft breezes. The conversation drifted here and there, but then the two lovers of wisdom began to discuss questions of epistemology, questions concerning the nature and limits of human knowledge.

One philosopher asked the other, "*Say, you know that old question—if a tree falls in a forest with no one around, does it make a sound?*" "*Sure,*" was the response, "*everybody knows that one.*" "*Well, what's the answer?*" "*Don't you know?*" asked the second philosopher. "*I wouldn't have asked if I did,*" said the first philosopher. "*Just think about it and then you'll see what the only certain answer can possibly be.*" At that instant, the two philosophers looked at each other and, as if lightning had struck, the first philosopher realized the answer. The answer is . . .

That's the end of the story you are reciting. After you finish the last sentence, "*The answer is . . .*", the curtain quickly drops. Can you imagine the reaction

DOI: 10.4324/9781003237150-16

from your audience? Wouldn't there be a huge uproar, people stomping and yelling, "*Well, What's the answer?*"

Now, let's add one small detail to this experiment. You have recited this story from memory. Also, you have recited it without any of your external senses functioning—in other words, you spoke the words without hearing them, you did not see your audience, you could not even feel the floorboards under your feet. Would you be able to answer the question: "How did the audience react to your story once it was concluded?"

The answer is: You couldn't really tell for sure how they reacted because you would have had no contact with them through any of your senses. You might guess how they would react, but that is not the question. The question asks whether you could *know* for sure how they reacted.

If this is the answer to the question about how the audience responded to your recitation of the story, can you see the answer to the question about the tree falling in the forest with no one around?

Well, the answers for the two questions are the same—You don't know! If a tree falls in the forest and no one is around to hear it, you do not know whether it makes a sound. This is the answer that the important Irish philosopher **George Berkeley** (pronounced "BARK-lee," as in former NBA great Charles Barkley) would have given to this question. (Berkeley lived from 1685 until 1753 and is usually referred to as "Bishop Berkeley" because he was a bishop in the Anglican Church.) So, in this case, there were *three* possible answers to the original question: "Yes", "no", and "unknown."

For Further Thought

1. An important principle in Berkeley's philosophy is "to be is to be perceived." In other words, we cannot be certain that anything really exists unless it is certain that this thing is being perceived. Can you think of a counterexample (See **Question #2**) that would refute this position? Thus, can you think of something that you know for certain will continue to exist even if it is not perceived by anyone? Be careful before you answer!

2. Think about the following questions:
   (a) What would happen if every human being went to sleep at the same time and, as a result, no one was perceiving the earth? Would the earth vanish?
   (b) What would happen if everything capable of perception—human beings, animals, and so forth—were to disappear from the earth? Again,

would the earth vanish? What would Berkeley say, based on "to be is to be perceived"?

(c) Could the earth have existed without supporting any type of conscious life? It seems so. How then could the earth have continued to exist if nothing was alive to perceive it? (Hint: Think about Berkeley's occupation and perhaps you can determine how he would argue for the existence of the earth even if no *human being* were alive to perceive it.)

"If the doors of perception were cleansed
everything would appear as it is, infinite."
William Blake, poet and painter

Question #15—David Hume

Are you certain that the law of gravity is really a law?

Do you have a pencil or pen in your hand? If you do and you let go of it, what would happen? Well, that's the easiest question in this book! The pencil would fall. Why? That's easy, too: Gravity causes it to fall. Simple, eh? But change the question a bit: Are you certain that the pencil will fall? Of course! Why are you certain? Well . . . because the law of gravity is a law. But, why are you certain that the law of gravity is a law?

Here are a series of statements about various possibilities. Before you read each statement, spend a moment thinking about what it means to be possible and what it means to be impossible. Then, answer "yes" or "no" in the space provided. It is possible that:

1. You could double your intelligence.   _____
2. You might be rich and famous.   _____
3. You could have been born on the other side of the earth.   _____
4. Acorns could start to grow into ears of corn
    (after all, "corn" is just "acorn" without an "a"!).   _____
5. Pencils could start to grow from seeds.   _____
6. Pencils would not fall when released.   _____

If you answered "yes" to any of these statements, you were thinking about possibility in a way which the Scottish philosopher **David Hume** (1711–1776) insists is perfectly reasonable. But even if you answered "yes" to some statements, perhaps you did *not* answer yes to 4–6. Why? If 1–3 represent possibilities, wouldn't statements 4–6 also be possible?

For Hume, we are certain that pencils must fall when released only because whenever we've seen a pencil (or anything—not counting balloons!) released, it

DOI: 10.4324/9781003237150-17

has fallen. But, is there anything impossible—or, as Hume would say, "contradictory"—about a pencil not falling once it's been released? Absolutely not. It would be very odd if this were to happen, but it would be, and certainly is, entirely possible.

If this point is granted, then Hume draws a powerful conclusion. He argues that events we see in nature could always be different from the way we have been accustomed to seeing them. So when we say that gravity is a causal "law," what we are really saying is that our experience has been such that we are in the habit of seeing things, when they are released, always fall toward the earth. As a result, the law of gravity amounts to just a record of ordinary experience. In this sense, it is not really a law at all. It's just the way things have always happened—at least so far.

For Further Thought

1. There are many types of law: federal, state, and local government, church (for the religious), and laws of nature. The laws of a government or church can always be changed. But, can the laws of nature? If not, then natural laws are very different from the laws humans make to govern themselves or regulate the observance of their religious beliefs.

2. Why would the laws of nature—the laws studied by science—differ from other types of law? And, since science is an ongoing form of study, why should we believe what science says about the laws of nature? Is the certitude provided by science any different from the certitude provided by common sense? If so, why? Hume's position makes us wonder about exactly what science has shown concerning the way the world functions.

". . . we receive but what we give—
And in our life alone does Nature live."
Samuel Taylor Coleridge, poet and philosopher

Question #16—Immanuel Kant

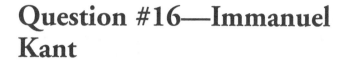

How can you tell when you know something?

"I know I'm right!"

Are you sure? And, if you are sure, why are you sure? Because it feels right to you or, perhaps, for some other reason? The question of how we can tell for certain that we know something has concerned philosophers for thousands of years.

The following exercises give you an opportunity to consider this problem:

1. Do you know that 2 + 2 = 4? How do you know?
    (Circle a, b, or c):

    a. It feels right when I look at it.
    b. I learned arithmetic in first grade.
    c. I realize that it can be proven using universally accepted mathematical principles.

2. You are holding a ripe, red apple. How do you know that it is red?
    (Circle a, b, or c)

    a. Because I can clearly see its redness.
    b. Because everyone calls this color "red."
    c. Because I can see that it is red—and it *is* red.

If you answered (c) to both questions, you are thinking about knowledge in the same way as **Immanuel Kant** (1724–1804). Kant is one of the most important philosophers of the modern era. In a long and difficult book, *The Critique*

53

DOI: 10.4324/9781003237150-18

of Pure Reason, Kant analyzes knowledge by describing conditions that must be satisfied before we can be said to know something.

For Kant, knowledge is attained when certain subjective and objective conditions occur. For example, if (a) you are not even slightly doubtful that something is true—if you are positively and *subjectively* certain of something and if (b) what you are certain about is *objectively* clear to everyone so that everyone can see it, then you can say that you "know" that this something is true. So knowledge, for Kant, must include both *subjective* and *objective* elements. If you review the two (c) answers given above, you will recognize that they both contain subjective and objective elements, that is, elements about both you as an observer and what it is you are observing.

For Further Thought

1. If, according to Kant, knowledge includes subjective and objective elements, what is the difference between knowledge and *opinion*? What is the difference between knowledge and *belief*? (These are both difficult questions. Hint: Think of a statement that is a belief and another statement that is an opinion and then ask yourself what is the difference between an opinion and a belief. If you can state that distinction, then try to distinguish between either an opinion or a belief and knowledge. Here are an opinion and a belief to test your abilities at this problem in epistemology, but feel free to use your own examples if you wish).

   Opinion: "It is my opinion that, although the earth might seem spherical, it is really flat."

   Belief: "I believe that history has shown that communism is a better form of government than democracy."

2. If you did *not* answer (c) to both questions in the activity, then you might disagree with Kant's position on the nature of knowledge. If you do disagree, can you say why?

"All knowledge is of itself of some value. There is nothing so minute or inconsiderable that I would not rather know it than not."
Samuel Johnson, author and lexicographer

Question #17—Ludwig Wittgenstein

Can another person understand your feelings?

"I'm so sad."
"I know just how you feel."

You probably have been on both sides of this exchange—feeling sad about something yourself and, at other times, offering sympathy to someone who is experiencing sadness.

Consider this situation: You studied hard for an important exam, but you did not get a good grade. Which of the following reactions would most likely apply to you? (Circle the most appropriate answer.)

(a) sadness
(b) disappointment
(c) frustration
(e) anger

It is possible, of course, that your reaction might be a combination of the above responses. But, assume that you are mainly sad. When you say you are "sad," what happens when someone hears you say that word? You can feel sad and someone can see how you look when you say you feel sad, but can someone feel sad the way you feel sad? Should you assume that another person can feel an emotion the way you feel that emotion?

The important 20th-century philosopher **Ludwig Wittgenstein** (1889–1951) made a careful study of language and its connections to mind and to the way we feel. In his work *Philosophical Investigations*, he frequently used the concept of a "language game" to help explain what happens when we speak. This is not a game understood as an activity that people might participate in for fun. Wittgenstein thought that when we speak a natural language (such as English or Spanish), we

DOI: 10.4324/9781003237150-19

55

obey certain rules that control when that language will be considered meaningful.

As a result, when we express our feelings in words, there are certain ways in which words referring to sadness will be used, as well as certain actions or gestures which are appropriate to those words. If I said *"I feel sad"* while laughing or while doing cartwheels of joy, I would not be using the word "sad" correctly; I would not be playing the language game of sadness according to the rules.

Also, if I said *"I feel happy when I'm sad,"* that would also not be playing according to the rules since, under normal circumstances, we could not say that we felt sad and happy at the same time. Our audience would become confused and not know what we had in mind to say. So, rather than claim that we have direct insight into the way another person feels because we can somehow inhabit their minds, what we do is participate in language games. And, since all of us "play" these games, we all have some sense of what everyone means when they use words in a certain way.

Try to think of words or phrases that will express the way you feel when you experience basic emotions. Use the spaces below for your ideas on this subject. (One reason poetry is so effective is because it can evoke feelings in ways that the language of prose cannot, or at least not with the same kind of precision and depth. Here philosophers must let poets take a bow!)

When I am sad, I feel like _____
_____

When I am sad, I am _____
_____

When I am happy, I feel like _____
_____

When I am happy, I am _____
_____

For Further Thought

1. Can you think of evidence that demonstrates with absolute certainty that there are other minds that can see and feel the way your mind does? In fact, can you "see" or "hear" another mind? Do you believe that computers function as if they had minds (see **Question #20**)?

2. Ask a group of people, perhaps an entire class, to contribute their thoughts on how to show the feeling of sadness or some other basic feeling. Then, have the class discuss the various contributions and see what reasons are given for selecting one version as more "accurate" or "vivid" than another.

3. Is language the best way to express our emotions? Would the arts of music or painting represent emotions more vividly and truly? Select a work of music or a work of art (painting, sculpture, and so forth) and analyze whether or not this work expresses emotions better than language.

"The heart has its reasons which reason does not understand."
Blaise Pascal, mathematician and philosopher

Question #18—Jean-Paul Sartre

Can you lie to yourself?

Telling a lie is usually not difficult. People who tell lies do so for many reasons, one of which is—or so they would like to think—to escape from a difficult situation. Whether it is ever appropriate to tell a lie is discussed in **Question #7**. But, even if times exist when there would be some reason to tell a lie to another person, can we ever lie to ourselves?

Example A:

Let's say that the "coolest" kids in school are going to do something that they all say they like to do, but that you don't like to do. However, it would be neat to belong to the cool group. And then, you're invited to go with them! So, if you do what they do, then you'll be as cool as they are!

Review the following possible outcomes of your participation in (you select the activity—remember, the cool kids like to do it; you do not). Then, circle the experience that you believe would be most likely to occur if you did participate in this activity:

1. I discover that I do enjoy it after all.
2. I don't enjoy it but I can pretend to others that I do.
3. I don't enjoy it but I can pretend to myself that I do.
4. I don't enjoy it but I can believe that I do even if I am still aware of the fact that I do not.

Example B:

Your friends smoke, and they urge you to do so, as well. In order to keep these people as your friends, you light your first cigarette. Then, you take your first puff. Here are three reactions you might have to your first experience with smoking. Indicate which one of these three would most likely happen for you:

58

DOI: 10.4324/9781003237150-20

1. You tell yourself—"I really do like it!"—while you furiously hack and cough.
2. Ugh, I can't stand it, but I won't admit this reaction to my friends who are smokers.
3. I don't enjoy it. But, if I tell myself often enough that I do enjoy it when I'm doing it, then perhaps I will eventually make myself enjoy it even during the time when I know that I do not enjoy it.

The French philosopher, **Jean-Paul Sartre** (1905–1980), was one of the most important figures in the 20th-century philosophical movement known as *Existentialism*. Many philosophers were called Existentialists, and they often differed widely among themselves on many issues. However, they shared the belief that philosophy should think about the concrete, ordinary experiences of our everyday existence.

In a long book called *Being and Nothingness*, Sartre (pronounced "Sart") analyzes a number of aspects of ordinary human life. One of these aspects he called *bad faith*. We are in bad faith whenever we lie to ourselves, that is, when we somehow convince ourselves that something is true even when we know, deep down, that it is not. If, for instance, you selected either (4) for *Example A* or (3) for *Example B* (or, perhaps, both of these answers), then you have some idea what it would mean to be in bad faith according to Sartre's definition of this concept.

In order to remove ourselves as far away from bad faith as possible, it is essential that we know as much about ourselves as we can. According to tradition, the words "know thyself" were inscribed on the temple to the divine oracle in the time of the early Greeks, the era of Plato and Aristotle. But, such self-knowledge is usually difficult to attain. One constant problem is that we tend to mix up the things we believe we *want* with the things we really and truly *need*. We do so to such an extent that people who can truthfully say that they know themselves are rare—and to be admired for their effort and insight. How well do you know yourself?

For Further Thought

1. Can you think of an example when you have been in bad faith, that is, when you have lied to yourself about something? What would be the best way to deal with this situation?

2. Is it possible that we are always in some sense in bad faith? Do you think it is possible for human beings to be completely honest with themselves about everything they are and do?

"We lie loudest when we lie to ourselves."
Eric Hoffer, longshoreman and philosopher

Question #19—Bertrand Russell

Do you perceive things as they are or only as they seem to be?

Knowing about yourself can be difficult. But, what about knowing something other than yourself?

Let's take what appears to be a simple example—a desk or chair will do. If we know that the desk is indeed a desk, we must begin with what we can see, feel, touch, and so forth. So knowing that the desk is a desk begins with perceiving a certain object *as* a desk.

Try this experiment. Two people, you and a friend or classmate, look at a desk. You stand directly over the top of the desk, your friend looks at it from across the room. Now each of you describe *exactly* what you see. Remember, describe only what you see, what you are actually perceiving. In the spaces below, describe the object's (a) size, (b) shape, and (c) color:

Person A: Person B:

a.   a.

b.   b.

c.   c.

Do both of you have the same visual experience? You will describe an object that has a certain size; the other person will describe an object of a different, somewhat smaller size (since the distance from your friend to the object is greater). What about its shape? You will see the shape as a rectangle, the other observer will see the shape as a rhombus (since the angle of observation is different). The two of you might also describe the object as having different shades of color (if, for example, the room is lit and the light casts a glare on the object being analyzed).

Bertrand Russell (1872–1970), eminent mathematician and philosopher, says in *The Problems of Philosophy* that, strictly speaking, we know only the informa-

DOI: 10.4324/9781003237150-21

tion given through our senses, such as the color, shape, and feel of an object. So, when we see things, we are not directly in touch with them, but only with our own experience of these things. Philosophers, Russell included, have called these experiences "sense-data" ("data" is plural, from the Latin; the singular is "sense-datum"). Sense-data are, therefore, whatever information is "given to the senses."

But, since people have different sense-data of the same object, it becomes a problem whether these sense-data refer to the same thing. After all, since sense-data differ, why should any one person's experience be more special than any other person's? In fact, how do we know that the object we are looking at is indeed really the *same* object for everyone?

It seems then that, although we might be able to reason to the fact that it is the same object, we cannot perceive that it is the same object. What each person perceives is private to that person. These sense-data belong only to one person, and it is possible that they differ from the perceptions of every other person. In fact, and even more strange, how can we be certain that what our senses tell us refers to an existing object in the first place?

This is one way to approach the problem of *appearance* and *reality*. What appears to us through our senses certainly might be real, but how do we know that such appearances do indeed refer to reality? Many philosophers have taken this problem very seriously since the answer to this question will determine (a) what sorts of things a philosopher will count as real and (b) what sorts of things only appear to be real, but are not.

And you thought there was nothing mysterious and intriguing about looking at a simple, ordinary desk!

For Further Thought

1. What sort of evidence can be used to determine what is and is not real? For example, are numbers real (see **Question #23**)? Are thoughts real? Are thoughts real in the same way that numbers are real (see **Question #24**)?

2. If you were to examine the desk with a microscope, what would you see? Are these sense-data more reliable in revealing what the desk is than what you can see by looking at the desk with your own eyes?

"All the mighty world of eye, and ear,—
both what they half create, and what perceive."
William Wordsworth, poet

Question #20—Daniel Dennett

Can computers think?

We know that computers are amazing machines. But, can computers think? This question has been and continues to be widely discussed, especially as computers become more complex and are able to perform more functions. The issue is one aspect of the rapidly growing field of Artificial Intelligence (or, to use its common abbreviation, AI).

The answer to the question "Can computers think?" depends on the meaning of the concept of thinking. If we knew what it meant for a human being to think, it would seem to be a simple matter to decide whether a computer can think. Unfortunately, what it means for a human being to think is also widely discussed—and the subject of considerable disagreement. These discussions, and disputes, occur not only among philosophers, but also for cognitive scientists and a number of other scientific disciplines that study the brain and its activities.

The following activity will introduce you to how complex—and fascinating—this question is. Read the five opinions about the possibility of computers thinking and check "true" or "false" in the space provided.

Computers can think *if*:

a. A computer beats the world's champion at chess.　　T ____　F ____
b. A computer writes poetry.　　T ____　F ____
c. A computer writes a novel as long as—and as
　good as—Leo Tolstoy's *War and Peace*.　　T ____　F ____
d. A computer makes itself move.　　T ____　F ____
e. A computer says, and says accurately, "I'm sad."　　T ____　F ____

The philosopher **Daniel Dennett** (1942–) argues that we ought to replace the concept of "thinking" with "consciousness." So, for Dennett, the question is

DOI: 10.4324/9781003237150-22

whether computers are conscious in the way human beings are conscious. Then, the problem becomes how to explain human consciousness.

Dennett addresses this question by reversing the usual direction of questions about AI. Instead of asking a human being to imagine whether or not a computer can be conscious, Dennett argues that our wondering should be in the opposite direction: Is the way human beings are conscious any different from the way computers are "conscious" while they whir and hum, doing all manner of useful and creative things?

This is a complicated question. Answering it will require us to think about the reality of the computer as a machine compared to the reality of a human being as a living organism. In fact, this question is just one of many questions that depend upon how we understand reality. Are you ready for another journey in our philosophical odyssey—this one venturing into new, strange, and fascinating territory?

For Further Thought

1. Five different types of mental behavior were given in the activity section of this question. If you were the author of this activity, would you include any other types of mental behavior that you believe are essential for a computer to perform in order to prove that computers are conscious and can think?

2. Science is learning more and more about the brain. Will there come a time when science can explain *every* type of human feeling, emotion, thought, and desire in terms of brain activity? If not why not? What do human beings do that *cannot* ultimately be explained in terms of the way the brain functions?

"If automation keeps up, man will atrophy all his limbs but the push-button finger."
Frank Lloyd Wright, architect

PART III

Reality

Are you real? Of course. Are trees real? Of course. Are numbers real? Of course. Are you, trees, and numbers all real in the same way?

Does your skin have a certain color? Yes. Is that color real? Yes. Are you real in the same way the color of your skin is real?

You are a human being. Your friends are human beings. Both you and your friends certainly exist. But, does the class "human being" exist by itself, apart from individual human beings?

These are the kind of questions philosophers pose when they are thinking about reality. This area of philosophy is called **Metaphysics**, and it is the most abstract—and also, for many philosophers, the most interesting—type of philosophical inquiry. In this section, you will be introduced to some of the classic questions that have intrigued metaphysicians for thousands of years. In a way, questions about values (Part I) and questions about knowledge (Part II) are all rooted in questions about reality. After all, what you think is real will certainly affect your values and what you believe you can know about the world—and about yourself.

The questions in Part III are especially challenging—be prepared to think, but don't forget to enjoy yourself while you do so!

"Metaphysics is the attempt of the mind
to rise above the mind."
Thomas Caryle, historian

65

Question #21—Parmenides

Can you think about nothing at all?

A variation on this question is sometimes used as a mental puzzle. If you try not to think of something, then it becomes very difficult *not* to do exactly that. In spite of your best efforts, part of your mind keeps returning to what another part of your mind is telling you it doesn't want to think about!

Instead of asking your mind not to think about something, ask it to think about absolutely *nothing*. Try it! Is your mind imagining a black void, a large empty region of space? Is that nothing? No! It's empty space, and the darkness and emptiness certainly do exist. So, it seems that the answer to the question at the top of this page is "no."

The early Greek philosopher **Parmenides** (c. 515–445 B.C.) tried to think about nothing and also about the word *not*, which we often use as a negative term in ordinary sentences. But, Parmenides reasoned that, if we think about nothing, then nothing becomes something. Why? Because nothing must become something, otherwise we would not be able to think about it. So, if nothing must become something in order to be thought about, then it seems that we cannot think about nothing. Therefore, Parmenides concluded, nothing does not exist at all!

This conclusion seems odd. For if nothing does not exist, then neither does "not." But, if "not" does not exist, then any statement containing a "not" (e.g., "Athens is not New York") becomes meaningless. Parmenides faced this consequence bravely—he reasoned that *all reality is one* and that any apparent differences between things are merely illusions.

What is happening here? Is there another way to approach the question of how to think about nothing? Yes, there is.

Imagine that you are taking a true/false examination made up by a philosopher with a rather unusual sense of humor. Here is the first question of the exam:

DOI: 10.4324/9781003237150-24

1. Answer "true" or "false" in the space provided:

This word has four letters.   _____

Well . . . ? If you are puzzled about the answer, there is good reason to be puzzled. The sentence says, "This word has four letters." But, what word? It is not clear to what word this sentence is referring. If "This word has four letters" refers to "word," then the sentence is true. But if "This word has four letters" refers to "has," then the sentence is false.

After we patiently point out this ambiguity, the philosopher revises the target sentence (the question remains the same):

1a. Answer "true" or "false" in the space provided:

The word "word" has four letters.   _____

In this case, the first occurrence of word *refers to* the second occurrence of "word" (the instance in quotation marks). Once the terms in the sentence function in this way, the *meaning* of the sentence becomes clear, and it is possible to answer the question accurately.

Let's apply the important distinction between *meaning* and *reference* to the original question of this chapter. When you think about "nothing," are you thinking about the meaning of the word "nothing," or are you thinking about what the concept of "nothing" refers to?

If you think about "nothing" as a concept, it refers to an idea with a certain nature or structure. So, "nothing" as a concept becomes like the concepts of "something" or "everything." And, since you now know that "nothing" can refer to a definite concept, you are in a position to think about the meaning of "nothing." You can locate "nothing" as an idea in your mind and focus attention on its meaning.

It seems then that we can avoid the kind of world Parmenides thought was real, a world where nothing does not exist in any sense, by distinguishing between what nothing means and what nothing refers to. (But, wait a moment, don't forget about Parmenides just yet! If you want to see a fascinating paradox constructed by the philosopher Zeno, a student of Parmenides, to show that Parmenides' position on the nature of reality is indeed true, see **Question #11**.)

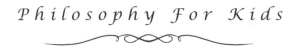

*". . . and nothing is
but what is not."*
William Shakespeare, poet and playwright

For Further Thought

1. The distinction between meaning and reference is very important in philosophy. Can there be meaningful sentences about things that do not exist, that is, when the sentence does not refer to anything real? Thus, is it meaningful to say "*All centaurs have four legs*" if, in fact, centaurs do not exist?

2. As you have no doubt noticed, this question is especially challenging—and so is the following deceptively sneaky question! See what kind of metaphysician you are: Consider the sentence "*Athens is not New York*" and ask yourself, can I explain how the word *not* functions in this sentence?

3. Is zero the same as nothing? Zero is now taken for granted in arithmetic, but for centuries the concept of zero was unknown, and its lack caused difficulties in elementary mathematical contexts. If zero and nothing are not the same, how do you know the difference between these two realities?

Question #22—Democritus

Does anything ever happen by chance?

"Chance is a word void of sense;
nothing can exist without a cause."
Voltaire, author and philosopher

We often use "chance" to explain unexpected or unusual events. Sometimes, chance events help us, sometimes they are harmful, sometimes neither. The following activity will give you an opportunity to think about chance—and to appreciate how mysterious the concept of chance really is. If you think the following are events that happen by chance, answer "yes." If you think they are not chance events, answer "no."

1. Going to a movie and meeting someone
   you have not seen for a long time.   _____
2. Spraining your ankle while running.   _____
3. Winning the Lottery.   _____
4. Having a long and happy life.   _____
5. The sun exploding on the day after tomorrow.   _____

The Greek philosopher **Democritus** (c.460–c.370 B.C.) asserted that reality consisted of atoms (the English word *atom* is from the Greek *atomos*, meaning indivisible, that is, incapable of being divided into smaller parts). Thus, Democritus was a *materialist*, a metaphysical position in which reality is thought to consist in nothing but matter.

For Democritus, atoms were infinite in number, in constant motion, and they always existed. Furthermore, the atoms moved about and clung together to form bodies, all the bodies that exist in nature, including humans. This process occurred mechanically, without purpose or design. So if a living thing died or a

DOI: 10.4324/9781003237150-25

69

nonliving thing broke into parts, their various atoms simply moved away and became elements in other beings.

If you answered "yes" to *any* of the five events listed in the activity, Democritus would disagree. For him, *all five* of those events—even the sun exploding the day after tomorrow—happen according to mechanical principles. For Democritus, things never happen just "by chance."

In fact, a "chance" event only shows our ignorance of prior conditions of the atoms composing that event. If we knew everything about where the atoms were going and what was moving them to go there, then *nothing* would appear to occur by chance. *Chance* is a synonym for *ignorance—our* ignorance of how atoms move about the universe.

For Further Thought

1. If Democritus is right, then each person is simply a group of atoms moving—and acting—by mechanical principles. How then can you be praised or blamed for your actions? For it seems as if everything has been determined—whatever you have already done and will do in the future.

2. Democritus denies that there are chance events because of his interpretation of reality. How would reality have to be described in order to allow for the possibility of chance events? (This is a difficult question. Try it only if you feel philosophically adventurous!)

3. Do you think Democritus must explain why atoms seem to keep forming things *of the same class*? Why wouldn't atoms just keep forming things in such a way that there were no classes of things at all? In other words, where every single thing is different from every other single thing?

4. Will science ever reach a point where we will know everything there is to know about nature? Give reasons to support your answer.

"A throw of the dice will never eliminate chance."
Stéphane Mallarmé, poet

Question #23—Plato

What happens to numbers when you are not using them?

"I invent nothing. I discover."
Auguste Rodin, sculptor

Almost everyone knows something about mathematics. After all, arithmetic, one of the most basic areas of mathematics, is essential for many practical situations in ordinary life. Arithmetic uses numbers and combines them in various ways. But, have you ever wondered what happens to numbers when no one is thinking about them?

The following is a multiple-choice exercise. Circle a, b, or c, whichever you think best describes what happens to numbers when you are not using them or thinking about them in any way:

a. Nothing happens to them: 2 + 2 *always* equals 4 whether people think about it or not.
b. The numbers vanish—numbers exist only when people use them.
c. As soon as numbers have been thought of by human beings, they exist by themselves, even when no one is thinking about them.

Although this question might seem somewhat odd, it is important from the standpoint of metaphysics. We believe that numbers are real. But, how are they real? If numbers and mathematical concepts—square, circle, square root, and so forth exist *only* as ideas, then these ideas begin to exist only when mathematicians create them. If, on the other hand, mathematical concepts exist by themselves, then mathematicians do not create these concepts, they discover them, just as early explorers discovered previously unknown continents that had existed there all the time.

In the dialogue called *Phaedo* (named after one of its characters), the Greek philosopher **Plato** (427–347 B.C.) argues that 2 is not the same as 1 + 1. Rather,

71

DOI: 10.4324/9781003237150-26

1 + 1 is something that "happens" to 2, but it is not *the same as* 2. For Plato, numbers are not just integers in a series. He thought that, although 2 and 3 were numbers, 2 was a different kind of number than 3, 3 was a different kind of number than 4, and so forth.

One way to understand Plato's approach to numbers is to think of the following simple computations in arithmetic:

$$4 - 2 = 2$$
$$3 - 1 = 2$$
$$1 + 1 = 2$$

The number 2 remains constant throughout these computations. Therefore, 2 itself is a distinct being, capable of being employed in all types of mathematics. For Plato then, numbers have *always* existed. Numbers do not need human minds thinking about them before they begin to exist. So, Plato would say that the correct answer to the activity is "a."

For Further Thought

1. Whether or not numbers exist by themselves, apart from minds thinking about them, is a disputed question in the *Philosophy of Mathematics*. Not all philosophers interested in these questions agree with the Platonic approach to numbers. Can you think of a way to explain the numbers used in arithmetic without saying, as Plato does, that they always existed?

2. When students are working with triangles (in geometry), are they thinking about figures that exist only when drawn on a surface, or are they thinking about a kind of reality that exists by itself and is known only by the mind? How would Plato have answered this question?

3. Another philosophical usage of arithmetic appears in **Question #13.**

"I have often admired . . . the secret magic of numbers."
Sir Thomas Browne, author and poet

Question #24—Aristotle

Are numbers and people equally real?

Are you real? Of course! Are you and a friend of yours real? Of course! Are numbers real? Of course! Are numbers real the way you are real? Hmmmmm.

At first glance, this last question might seem strange, but when philosophers study metaphysics, they ask many strange questions! They do this because, if anyone takes the time to think about reality, it becomes very mysterious—and endlessly fascinating. Is your reality as a human being any different than the reality of the number 2?

The following questions are unusual because they are abstract, so think for a moment about what is being asked before you answer "yes" or "no." Also, see whether you can detect the pattern in the sequence of questions.

1. Is a number more real than a human being?   _____
2. Is a human being more real than a dog?   _____
3. Is a dog more real than a plant?   _____
4. Is a plant more real than a stone?   _____
5. Is a stone more real than a snowflake?   _____
6. Is a snowflake more real than an atom?   _____
7. Is an atom more real than a subatomic particle?   _____
8. Is a subatomic particle more real than a centaur?   _____
9. Is a centaur more real than a square circle?   _____

If you answered "no" to all nine questions, then you would probably agree with the position in metaphysics that maintains that all real things are real in the same way. This position claims that the only alternative to what is real is nothing, or nonexistence (see **Question #21**). To talk about things being "more" or "less" real is simply a waste of mental energy that could be put to better philosophical use.

But, there is another way to look at reality. In a work called *Metaphysics*, the Greek philosopher **Aristotle** (384–322 B.C.) showed that "being can be said in

DOI: 10.4324/9781003237150-27

many ways." This principle means that the philosopher must take the time and effort to describe existing things in terms of *how* they are real and also whether degrees or levels of reality are real and meaningful. If you would like some practice in this kind of metaphysical thinking, read on.

For Further Thought

1. Does having a certain property make a thing more real than a thing that lacks that property? For example, if (as Plato thought—see **Question #23**), numbers are eternal, are numbers more real than you because you have a limited life span?

2. If one thing has more properties than another thing, is it more real? For example, are you more real than a stone just because you are more complex than a stone?

3. The pattern in the nine questions moves from something abstract—a number—to a being that is very complex—a human—downward through decreasing levels of complexity and size, to a mythical being, then to a square circle, which, because it is contradictory, does not exist at all (for this sense of impossibility, see **Question #30**). Can this pattern help you determine whether any of the beings referred to in the nine questions are "more" or "less" real than any of the other beings?

"Human kind cannot bear very much reality."
T. S. Eliot, poet

Question #25—St. Augustine

Is time what you see when you look at a clock?

"It's time to go to school."
"It's time for dinner."
"Time to do your homework!"

Everyone has wondered at some point about what time it is, especially if something fun or exciting is about to happen, or if you are waiting for something unpleasant or boring to be over. But, have you ever wondered just what time *is*? This question is philosophical, very interesting, and, if you are willing to think about it long enough, very mysterious.

St. Augustine, who was born in North Africa and lived from 354 to 430 A.D., was a theologian and philosopher who thought that he could explain time, although he admitted that he often became confused when he tried to think about it. Here is a summary of ideas (taken from a work called *Confessions*) that are important to the way he thought about time:

What did you do yesterday? This is easy to answer. But now ask, "Where is yesterday?" Hmmmm. That one is not so easy. One answer would be: It is gone and it won't return.

Ask yourself what you'll do tomorrow. You may have a few things in mind. Now ask, "Where is tomorrow?" That one is hard, too. We might say tomorrow isn't here yet. In fact, if we think about it, tomorrow will *never* be here. For as soon as tomorrow is here, it's not tomorrow, it's today!

Now ask yourself when you are reading this page. Well, you are reading it right now, in the present. But how do you know you are in the present? Only because you are aware of yourself looking at this page (or at something else). So, you know you are in the present whenever you are seeing, hearing, touching, or using any of your senses.

DOI: 10.4324/9781003237150-28

Here are more questions about time that you will enjoy thinking about and answering. Answer the next two questions either "yes" or "no."

1. Does a tree grow if no one is watching it? _____
2. Does time pass when you're asleep? _____

Now, circle the answers that seem best for the following questions:

3. When time passes, what does it feel like?

   a. Like riding along with the wind.
   b. Nothing—time doesn't feel like anything.
   c. It depends on what I'm doing.

4. What does time feel like when you're bored?

   a. Like trying to wiggle out of a tar pit.
   b. Like nothing—time doesn't feel like anything.
   c. Like being stuck watching a movie when the film breaks.

5. What does time feel like when you're having fun?

   a. Like flying down a hill on a sled during winter.
   b. I don't know—it passes so quickly.
   c. Who cares as long as we're having fun?

Review your answers to questions 1 and 2. Now, compare your answers for questions 4 and 5. It seems that time will "feel" very differently in the mind of the person answering question 4 than it will in the mind of the person answering question 5. And yet, the same person—you, for example—can be bored at one time and having fun at another time. The magic word here is, of course—time! Just what exactly is time?

St. Augustine thought that if time is divided into past, present, and future, then the past and the future, in a sense, don't exist. As he put it, the past is "no longer" and the future is "not yet."

Time seems to be vanishing right before our eyes! But wait, all we have to do is think about the present in the correct way and we will, it seems, understand time. Ask yourself, when do you have a *memory*? The answer is now, in the present. Although whatever you are remembering happened in the past, the memory you are having of the past is in your mind right now. Try it—remember the last time you did something that was fun. When are you remembering what you did? Right now!

Ask yourself, how do you know there will be a tomorrow? Well, you can't be absolutely sure, but you certainly expect there to be a tomorrow. When does this experience of *expectation* happen? Again, the answer is now, in the present. If you think about doing something fun tomorrow, you are expecting tomorrow to happen.

Now for the last of the three parts of time. Look at this sheet of paper. When are you looking at it? The answer is right now, in the present. You know that you are in the present because you are aware of your mind looking at the sheet of paper. So, when you are looking at something, you are aware that you are *perceiving* that thing.

Here is a summary of Augustine's philosophy of time. Augustine thought that time does not exist by itself; it is merely something the mind creates and then connects to some of the things your mind does. So, Augustine would say that the numbers you see on the face of a clock or on your wristwatch are *not* what time is: they are only numbers. They measure time as the numbers move along and change at a certain rate of speed. But, time itself is something else.

The past belongs with what you remember, the present with whatever you can perceive, the future with whatever you expect to happen. But all these activities are in your mind! Time exists only because of the way your mind works.

Do you think that this theory of time is true? One of the ways philosophers test their thinking is to imagine what conclusions would follow if they pretended that their thinking is true. Let's try this method with what Augustine has said about time.

Imagine the world being exactly the way it is now, but with one big difference: There are no minds, neither human nor animal. What would time be like in such a world? The answer is that *there would be no time*! Why? Because according to Augustine, time exists only in the mind. Therefore, on a world with no minds, there would be no time, since there would be no place for time to exist.

As you think about Augustine's ideas about time, be careful not to mix up time with things moving or growing (see **Question #11** for a fascinating discussion of how to understand motion). Plants, for example, will continue to grow on the world without minds because plants don't need minds in order to grow. If there is a tree in your backyard, do you need to think about it before it grows? Of course not! However, since neither you nor any other mind will observe this growth—remember that on our imaginary world there are no minds—then there will be no time to measure that growth. Therefore, for Augustine, there will be no time during which this growth occurs.

At this point, Augustine's thinking about time becomes very mysterious. Can you think of your own theory of time? Remember that in order for your theory to be different from Augustine's, it must not contain anything that includes the human mind.

For Further Thought

1. What would happen to time if all the clocks in the world suddenly stopped?

2. If time exists only in the mind, then whose mind is it in?

   (Perhaps you should set a limit on the time you spend trying to answer "What is time?" Good luck!)

*"There is no difference between time
and any of the three dimensions of space
except that our consciousness moves along it."*
H. G. Wells, author

Question #26—St. Thomas Aquinas

If the universe came from the Big Bang, where did the Big Bang come from?

How did the universe begin? According to the "Big Bang" theory, the universe originated about 20 billion years ago when a small amount of matter exploded and, over immense reaches of time, gradually formed the universe as we now know it. This is a basic theory in *cosmology*, the science studying the origin and structure of the universe (or "cosmos"). It is a theory held by many scientists who work in this field. But, will it explain everything that is relevant to the origin of the universe?

St. Thomas Aquinas (1225–1274) was one of the most important philosophers in the Middle Ages. He was also very influential in *theology*, the study of God and questions about God. Aquinas thought that the answers to some questions concerning God had to be accepted on religious faith alone. But he also thought that other questions about God could be demonstrated by reason and were, therefore, questions a philosopher could ask—and, perhaps, answer. One such question is: Can the existence of God be proven? Aquinas' answer: Yes!

In a work called the *Summa Theologica* (Latin for "highest theology"), Aquinas laid out five brief "ways" to show that God exists. The fifth way has been named the "Proof from Design," since Aquinas' reasoning is based on the fact that the universe appears to show order or design. The reasoning in this proof is subtle, but we can understand the main point of the fifth way—and also answer the above question about the Big Bang—by pretending that we live in a parallel universe existing "next door" to ours.

This universe is much like our own except that it is much older. It also has portals, windows in space, where we can watch events happening in the other universe—*our* universe! The portal we'll visit allows us to observe the dawn of

DOI: 10.4324/9781003237150-29

our universe, the very moment when, according to the Big Bang theory, our universe began. Of course, this visit is imaginary. So, let your imagination go to work . . . and also your ability to think and reason. As you gaze through the portal observing the birth of our universe, imagine that you are also circling the answer that best fits the following question:

1. What does the "stuff" of the Big Bang look like the instant before it explodes?

    a. Like a bulging watermelon.
    b. Like an unmoving geometrical object.
    c. Like a very complex bunch of stuff of no particular shape.

(Recall that you're watching the birth of the cosmos from a parallel universe that is older than our universe. If so, then the following question can be asked—just shift your position a bit at the portal.)

2. What did this stuff look like 1,000 years *before* it exploded?

    a. The same as it did just one second before it exploded.
    b. Completely different.
    c. Wait a minute—1,000 years earlier, the stuff that makes up the Big Bang did not exist!

You might have selected a or b, but answer c raises interesting philosophical questions (actually, so do answers a and b!); for now, however, let's explore answer c.

3. If the stuff of the Big Bang did *not* exist 1,000 years prior to the explosion, what *did* exist at that point?

    a. A bunch of other stuff, but stuff unrelated to the Big Bang.
    b. Nothing in our universe existed at that point.

Only two answers are given, but only two answers seem possible. However, answers a and b both lead to philosophical difficulties:

Answer a. If stuff did exist apart from whatever the Big Bang came from, then the universe existed before the Big Bang! The reason? This other stuff must be somewhere, and that "somewhere" must be the universe!

Answer b. If nothing existed before the stuff of the Big Bang went *bang!*, then the stuff of the Big Bang came from nothing. But how can something come from nothing? (Hmmm.)

4. One more question: If the stuff of the Big Bang did *not* exist 1,000 years before it exploded, where did this stuff come from?

   a. It could come only from a source other than itself.
   b. It just suddenly popped into existence.

Let's stop here. If, as you were wandering through this series of multiple-choice questions, you felt a bit like Alice trapped in an especially wacky Wonderland, then you probably have a good appreciation of the difficulty—and also the fascination—that philosophers have with this question. It is a very complex issue.

We'll try to clear things up just a bit. First, Thomas Aquinas lived 700 years before the Big Bang theory was thought of by scientists. But, if he were alive today, he would almost certainly ask the question that serves as the title of this chapter: "Where did the Big Bang come from?"

For Aquinas, something cannot come from nothing. This is simply impossible. Therefore, the stuff of the Big Bang must have been created; it cannot have just one day (could "days" have existed before the Big Bang [see **Question #25**]?) popped into existence.

Also, since Aquinas thought that the universe displays order, especially among those living beings that lack intelligence, such as plants and many types of animals, he reasoned that the creator of the stuff that became the universe must have been intelligent.

Finally, since the universe is very complex, this intelligence must have been extremely high; in a word, supreme. Therefore, only one being could have been such a creator. This being is God. So since the universe is both complex and orderly and since something cannot come from nothing, God must exist to create the universe—including the stuff of the Big Bang—and to give it the order it possesses. Notice that Aquinas has reasoned to the existence of God by considering natural things. He has not used *The Bible* or anything religious, only his ability to think and reason philosophically.

Finally, the answer Aquinas would give to the question "Where does the Big Bang come from?" is simple: It comes from God.

For Further Thought

1. If you were paying close attention to the multiple-choice questions, you might have noticed that an assumption was made in question 2, and a very important one at that. Perhaps you thought of it at the time; if so, then you are a very good philosopher! Can you see what Aquinas is assuming at that point in his argument?

2. Question 2 included as one of the possible answers that the stuff of the Big Bang did not exist 1,000 years prior to the Big Bang itself. But isn't it possible that matter, the stuff of the Big Bang, always existed? If it is in the nature of matter to be eternal, then matter always existed. But if matter always existed, then there is no need to ask where matter originated. Aquinas assumes that, since matter could not have come from itself, that matter must have been created. But if it is possible that matter is eternal, then matter always existed.

3. If matter is indeed eternal, what effect would this have on the conclusion of the fifth "way," the proof from design? Would eternal matter strengthen the conclusion of the fifth way—that there must be a God to create the order in the universe—or would it make this conclusion weaker?

   A final thought on this topic: The next time you read anything about the Big Bang, see whether the author, whoever it may be, discusses the problem outlined in this question: the origin of the Big Bang. Philosophy notices—and tries to answer—questions that many people either do not recognize as important or do not have the nerve to try to answer!

"The heavens declare the glory of God."
Psalms 19:1

Question #27—John Locke

Are you the same person you were five years ago?

Has a friend or relative who has not seen you for a while ever said, "*I didn't recognize you!*" Most of us have had this experience, especially when we are young and growing. Now, *you* know that you are you since *you* know that you are the same, even if five years (or more) have passed.

But, wait a minute, just how do you know for certain that you are you? After all, your cells are continually growing and dying and regrowing, your body is constantly changing in a variety of ways, your mind is always learning new information and having new experiences. And yet . . . you are still you. But why?

Philosophers call this the problem of "personal identity." They don't mean the kind of identity you can establish with a school I.D. card. That is just a plastic picture. In fact, the picture, in a way, misrepresents you since it does not change, and you are changing all the time. The problem is interesting and important because the solution will serve to establish what makes each of us an individual—*this* individual and not *that* individual.

What is the best way to determine that you are the same person? Review the following alternatives and circle the one which provides the best evidence that you are you:

1. Ask your parents or someone who has known you since birth.
2. Look at old photos of yourself.
3. Examine your birth certificate (to see whether your name is spelled correctly).
4. Remind yourself that you have always had the same body.

It seems that 2 and 3 are not very reliable, although 2 makes more sense than 3. We have already discussed 4; in fact, it is not entirely clear that you do have the same body. Same in what sense? You may have selected 1. Why? If your parents said that you are the same person they have raised since you were an infant, would that be certain evidence that it was still the same you? What

DOI: 10.4324/9781003237150-30

83

kind of evidence is their testimony? It is *external* evidence based on what they have perceived about you as a human being. There is no doubt that such evidence is worthwhile in many instances, but is it possible to establish your identity as *you* with a greater degree of certainty than that provided by what other people say?

The English philosopher **John Locke** (1632–1704), very influential for his political philosophy, was also important for his thoughts on knowledge and on the question of personal identity. In the *Essay Concerning Human Understanding*, Locke argues that our consciousness of ourselves establishes the strongest evidence that we have a personal identity. But, what kind of consciousness will best show that we are who we are?

Review the following types of consciousness and select the one that you think presents the strongest evidence that you are the same you that you always thought you were.

a. Your ability to know facts.
b. Your ability to perceive things in the world.
c. Your ability to speak.
d. Your ability to remember.

If you selected d, you agree with John Locke. Locke argued that our capacity for *remembering* events that happened to us will prove that we are and remain the same person over the passage of time. Even if our bodies are changing constantly, our memories of our past will remain the same memories. So, whenever you think back about something that happened to you, whether it was happy or sad or just routine, then, according to Locke, you are proving to yourself that you are really you!

For Further Thought

1. Some memories are vivid, others are weak. Does the fact that some of the events we remember are now a bit hazy weaken Locke's theory of personal identity?

2. If you thought that the testimony of your parents is the best way to prove that you are you, try your hand at **Question #19**. There you will confront reasons that will make you wonder whether people are indeed really perceiving what they believe they are perceiving.

"Learn to limit yourself, to content yourself with some definite thing, and some definite work; dare to be what you are, and learn to resign with a good grace all that you are not, and to believe in your own individuality."
Frédéric Amiel, essayist and philosopher

Question #28—Thomas Hobbes

Do you have a free will?

"Sir, we know our will is free, and there's an end on 't."
Samuel Johnson, author and lexicographer

(We are eavesdropping on a young person's thoughts.) "Let's see. I think I'll do a question in *Philosophy for Kids*. Most of them I've done, and they've been really interesting. Only a few left to try. I think I'll look at the one about this Thomas Hobbes dude. The question is, "Do you have a free will?" Well, of course I have a free will! I can choose to do the question on Hobbes or do something else. What could possibly be interesting about such a no-brainer? Sometimes these philosophers come up with the stupidest questions."

On the surface, the question "Do you have a free will?" might seem easily answered—"yes." At least we certainly believe we have a free will since it seems as if we are free to choose to do almost anything.

Let's consider some possibilities. Answer "true" or "false" in the space provided depending on whether or not you think you can will to do some—or all—of the following actions:

I can freely choose to:

a. Be a fair and just person.   _____
b. Be a good friend.   _____
c. Do my best in school.   _____
d. Tell a lie when it's useful.   _____
e. Cheat on a test.   _____
f. Become violent in a dispute.   _____
g. Be the richest person on earth.   _____
h. Be the greatest athlete ever.   _____
i. Rule the universe.   _____

DOI: 10.4324/9781003237150-31

You may have noticed the pattern in these nine examples. The first three, a, b, and c, are usually considered morally praiseworthy; these are good choices. The next three, d, e, and f, are morally blameworthy; these are not good choices. The final three, g, h, and i, are possible, but probably unrealistic.

You might not want to choose to do d–f; after all, if you get caught doing any of these actions, you will probably be punished. Similarly, you might not want to choose to do g–i since they represent what are, for most of us, unrealistic goals. But, the point is that you could choose to do *all nine* if you wished to do so. In this sense, then, it seems you *always* have a free will. It's just that some things that you could freely will to choose you would *not* choose to do. But, you always *could* have willed such a choice.

The question of this chapter seems easily answered. But, wait until we hear from a philosopher on the subject. **Thomas Hobbes** (1588–1679) was a very important figure in early modern political philosophy (as was John Locke—see **Question #27**). Hobbes also had strong views about human nature. One of his theories was that "will," as ordinarily understood in the concept of "free will," simply did not exist. Rather, whenever we choose to do something, what we call our "will" is simply the last desire or wish that moves us to act.

For example, I am thinking about whether or not to do a question in *Philosophy for Kids*. I deliberate about the matter—should I do this question or should I do something else? Prior to the moment when I make my choice, I believe that I could either (a) do the question or (b) do something else. But, Hobbes says, when I actually "will" to do something, some cause (or causes) makes me choose this action rather than some other action. In this case, I am more curious about what's happening in the question in *Philosophy for Kids* than I am about the other possible courses of action I could pursue. Therefore, my curiosity *causes* me to do the question on Thomas Hobbes.

The causes of what we will ourselves to do might be many things, and frequently we are unaware of their presence. But, if we had full knowledge of how our mind and body function, then we would always be able to know what we would choose to do. So, Hobbes concludes, there is no such thing as "free will." Rather, human beings are very complex organisms. And, although we might like to believe we can choose freely, in fact we are causally determined to make the choices that we finally select. So, for Hobbes, the answer to the question is "no," we do *not* have a free will. The reason is simply that the will does not really exist. It is a figment of the philosophical imagination.

87

For Further Thought

1. If Hobbes' position on free will is correct, does it make any sense to praise or blame people for what they do? Even if it is true that all our actions are caused, are we still responsible for what we do?

2. A related question: If all human actions are determined by causes, then is it fair to punish people for things they do? Can you think of a reason why, in society, it would still be just to punish people for doing certain actions?

3. Hobbes argues *explicitly* that free will is an illusion. A philosopher of a much earlier time has a theory about reality that *implies* that free will is an illusion—see **Question #22**.

"To enjoy freedom, we have to control ourselves."
Virginia Woolf, author

Question #29—Georg Hegel

Does anything depend on everything?

You exist. That is certain (but, since philosophers take nothing for granted, see **Question #13**). Do you need anything other than yourself in order to continue to exist? Yes. You need nature (to provide food and clothing), as well as other people (to provide friends, teachers, and so forth). But, how much "otherness" do you need in order for you to be you? In fact, is there a sense in which *the entire universe* must be taken into account before you are truly you? Does anything depend on everything?

This seems to be an especially wild idea, not to mention somewhat arrogant. But, see whether the theory that anything depends on everything might make sense after answering the following set of questions—each of which is about you! Put "yes" or "no" in the space provided:

Would you be different if:

    a. Your parents were different?   _____
    b. Your birth date was different?   _____
    c. Your native country was different?   _____
    d. The history of your native country was different?   _____
    e. The earth was different in terms of its natural laws?   _____
    f. The solar system was differently organized?   _____
    g. The universe was structured differently?   _____

If you answered "yes" to all or almost all of the seven questions, you are thinking about yourself as an individual in the same way that the German philosopher **Georg Hegel** (1770–1831) thought about individual things—*all* individual things, not just a particular human being. Hegel argues this position at great length (and in language that is difficult to read) in a work called *The*

DOI: 10.4324/9781003237150-32

Science of Logic. Hegel was one of the most impressive of all philosophers in terms of the remarkable breadth of his knowledge about the world and his ability to integrate that knowledge into an orderly and coherent system of concepts.

Think about it: Would each thing in the universe be different if its relations to any other thing in the universe were different? If the answer is "yes," then it makes sense to say that "anything depends on everything." No one thing can be understood by itself. Rather, anything and everything must be seen in the light of relations to everything else.

For Further Thought

1. It is not humanly possible to know everything there is to know about all the things that exist in the world. Does this circumstance refute Hegel's claim that anything depends on everything? (This is not an easy question. Spend time thinking about it before you try to answer. The pattern underlying the sequence of yes/no questions in the activity might provide you with a clue.)

2. In **Question #12**, Aristotle argues for a theory of truth based on the "correspondence," or correlation, between a proposition and a fact in the world. What would Hegel say about this theory of truth since, for him, everything is related to everything else?

   Here is an example that might help: For Aristotle, "Human beings are by nature two-legged" is a true proposition because it is a fact that, by nature, human beings have two legs. Would Hegel agree that we have said something *completely* true about human beings just because we can say the *single* proposition "Human beings are by nature two-legged"?

"To see a world in a grain of sand."
William Blake, poet and painter

Question #30

Are impossible things ever possible?

Quickly—get a pencil or pen. Take this quiz *right now*! Write "yes" or "no" in the space provided. Is it possible:

1. That you will live to be 75 years old? _____
2. That you will become rich? _____
3. That you will become famous? _____
4. That you will become rich and famous? _____
5. That you will win the Nobel Prize in literature? _____
6. That 3 + 2 = 6? _____
7. That the universe will disappear when you turn the page to the next chapter in *Philosophy for Kids*? _____
8. For a ball to be green and red all over? _____
9. For a sentence to be both true and false at the same time and in the same respect? _____

Is it possible for you to become another Michael Jordan or Albert Einstein or Julia Roberts? Of course. There is no telling what people can do if they work hard to realize their potential. However, it is also true that each of us has certain limits beyond which, it seems, it is not possible to go. Determining what these limits are is one of the great adventures in life. In fact, this adventure lasts an entire lifetime since, regardless of our age and what we have already accomplished, we can always try harder to realize something in ourselves that may have been hidden.

Becoming something wonderful or great in life represents one kind of possibility. Sometimes, we say that such possibilities are possible "in theory," even if they may not be possible "in fact." What does this distinction mean?

It may not be possible *in fact* for you to become another Michael Jordan because your body might not be as physically gifted, but it is possible *in theory*,

DOI: 10.4324/9781003237150-33

meaning that there is nothing contradictory about you being the next Michael Jordan.

It is possible, after all, that tomorrow you might meet a genie who would grant you one wish—and you wish to become the next Michael Jordan (or Albert Einstein, or Julia Roberts, and so forth). It would, however, be unwise to expect to meet a genie who would grant you this kind of wish. In fact, it would be unwise to expect to meet a genie, period. But, there is nothing impossible— in theory—about such a wondrous event occurring. So, in this case, something that may be impossible *in fact* (your becoming the next Michael Jordan) is still possible *in theory*.

Now that we know the distinction between possibility in theory and possibility in fact, let's review your answers to the quiz:

Question 1. Stay healthy and you'll probably live longer than that.
Questions 2–5. Yes—if you work hard, are fortunate, and are highly gifted.
Question 6. Why not shift the base to something other than 10? (For another, and very odd, way 3 + 2 does not equal 5, see **Question #13**.)
Question 7. Is it possible? Yes! But it's not at all likely. (Still, be careful when you turn that page!)
Question 8. No—how could a ball be both red and green all over?
Question 9. Absolutely not! This possibility is a contradiction and therefore it is not even theoretically possible.

To explain: A *contradiction* is a statement that is necessarily false. For example, if one said "This ball is red and this ball is not red," that proposition is a contradiction. It is necessarily false because of what the proposition tries to assert about the ball being simultaneously both red and not red. We will never experience a contradiction in any way. In fact, it is not even theoretically possible for what is referred to in a contradiction to exist. So, some impossible things (in fact) are possible (in theory), but other impossible things (in theory, e.g., contradictions) are just that: impossible.

The answer to the original question? It depends. If the impossible things are possible in fact, then the answer is "yes"; but, if the impossible things are impossible in theory, then the answer is "no."

The area in philosophy that studies this kind of impossibility is called *logic*. If you want to pursue additional explorations in logic and in the kind of thinking that is associated with logic, then turn the page. (But, turn it carefully! Remember question 7. . . .)

For Further Thought

1. We frequently hear the proposition "Anything is possible." If you were to evaluate that proposition philosophically, what would you say about it?

2. Thinking and writing in such a way as to produce a contradiction is one of the worst things that can happen to a philosopher. Why? (Hint: Take a simple example of a contradiction, such as the one in the discussion about a ball being both red and not red, and then ask: Can such a ball exist?)

3. Different people can realize different kinds of possibilities. Some people succeed in one area, some succeed in others. But, throughout this process and whatever area you pursue, you will always be you. Or will you? In fact, how do you know that you are you? See **Question #27** for a philosophical perspective on this intriguing question.

> *"The difficult we do immediately,*
> *the impossible takes a little longer."*
> U.S. Armed Forces motto

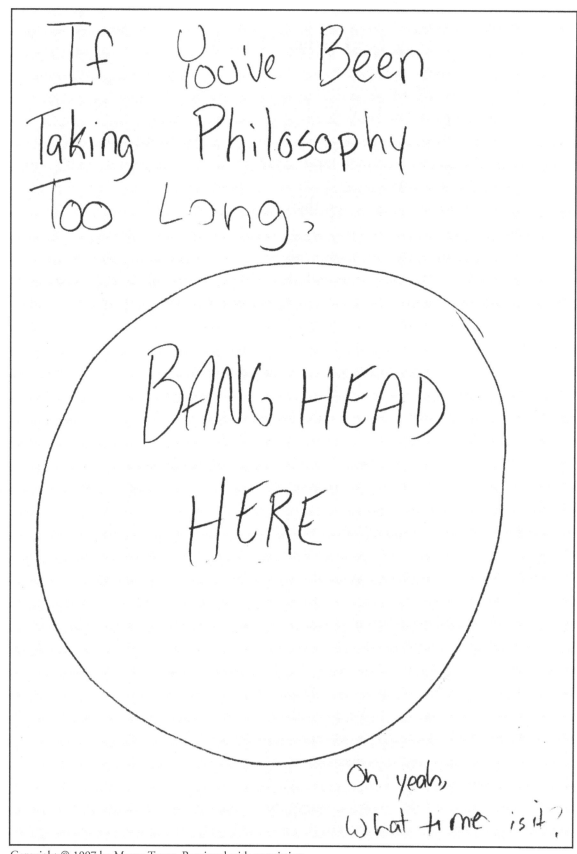

The opposite page is a representation of a sharply depicted, if spare, diagram, with accompanying message, that was presented to me by an eighth-grade student during a summer philosophy course at Northwestern University's Center for Talent Development. The class had been studying Augustine on time (see **Question #25**), and this young lady, extremely bright and articulate, had been vigorously arguing—although without visible success—against Augustine's theory that time exists only in the mind. I keep the drawing at home and often gaze at it, especially since the urge to do head-banging of my own is an all too frequent occupational hazard. Philosophy can be exhausting, as well as exhilarating.

PART IV

Critical Thinking

"To think is to live."
Cicero, orator and essayist

Human beings think. And human beings are thinking almost all the time. Most of our thinking we do correctly. But not all of it. And, unfortunately, those times when we are not thinking correctly are often precisely the times when we *should* be thinking correctly!

The area of philosophy that studies correct thinking is called **Logic**. Logic may be defined as the science of correct and incorrect reasoning. It is important to analyze incorrect reasoning so that we can recognize such reasoning *as* incorrect. The ability to evaluate reasoning, to know when reasoning has been done correctly and when it has made errors, is often referred to as "critical thinking."

The questions in Part IV include activities that will help you to know what it means to reason correctly and also how to become a better critical thinker. These activities, and the ability to think critically, are essential, not only in philosophy but in virtually every kind of study or subject—not to mention in the practical matters of daily life. Regardless of what you are interested in and what kind of life you lead, you will have to be able to think and reason correctly about your situation and the choices you face. The 10 questions in Part IV will give you a head start in acquiring the vitally important habits required to be a successful thinker.

Thinking can be hard work. But, it can also be interesting and fun (as you have seen from the earlier chapters in this book). So, have fun with the "logical" chapters that follow!

"Reading furnishes the mind only with the materials of knowledge; it is thinking makes what we read ours."
John Locke, philosopher

Question #31

Is it important to speak and write so you can be understood?

We speak and write for many reasons. One of the most important reasons is to communicate what we are thinking and feeling to other people. It is essential, therefore, to be able to think, speak, and write our thoughts as clearly as possible so that we can be understood. Sometimes, this clarity is easy to achieve. Other times, however, it is difficult and requires attention and practice.

Although it is often fun to play with words and have them do strange and interesting things, sometimes words can play tricks on us when we don't want them to do so. Consider the following statement: "*We should not speak ill of our friends.*" Is this statement true or false? Surely almost everyone would say that it is true. Aristotle would agree, as well, since if we were to speak ill of our friends, then we would not be showing them good will—an essential element in the definition of friendship (See **Question #2**). And, if we did speak ill of our friends, we would risk losing their friendship.

It is important to notice, however, that the statement "*We should not speak ill of our friends*" changes its meaning depending on *what* the speaker is thinking and *how* the speaker says the statement. Using your imagination, you should be able to recognize at least five ways in which the original statement will mean something different depending on shifting the emphasis when pronouncing various words in the sentence.

Read the five versions of the statement listed below either silently to yourself or aloud to a friend or classmate, emphasizing the *italicized* word in each version. Ask yourself (or a friend) what the statement means for each of the five different versions. Briefly write the difference in meaning in the space provided underneath each additional version of the statement.

1. "We should not speak ill of our *friends*."

DOI: 10.4324/9781003237150-35

2. "We should not speak ill of *our* friends."

_____

3. "We should not *speak* ill of our friends."

_____

4. "We *should* not speak ill of our friends."

_____

5. "*We* should not speak ill of our friends."

_____

This example (developed from *Introduction to Logic*, 10th ed. by Irving M. Copi and Carl Cohen) illustrates how easy it is to be misleading simply by overemphasizing one word in a statement. We can also make the same mistake when we write statements. It should be clear that we must be just as careful about what we write as about what we think and say.

For Further Thought

There are many ways to confuse people—or ourselves—when we are not clear about what we say and how we say it. Some of these ways are *fallacies*, or logical mistakes. We make these mistakes when we speak or write without thinking clearly and carefully. Several common fallacies are examined later (**Questions #33, #35, #36,** and **#37**). These questions will help you avoid logical mistakes in your own thinking and writing, as well as allow you to recognize such errors in the thinking and writing of others.

"Everything that can be thought at all can be thought clearly.
Everything that can be said can be said clearly."
Ludwig Wittgenstein, philosopher

Question #32

Should you always listen to the opinions of others?

"They who listen understand."
African proverb

We learn in many ways: by reading, thinking, observing what is going on around us, and also by talking to other people. Socrates spent a lot of time talking to other people (**Question #1**), but he spent just as much time listening to them. He did this because he thought that he could learn from them about many important things. For Socrates, this meant listening and, of course, thinking about what people had said to him.

We will hear a large assortment of opinions throughout the course of our lives. The following are opinions that you may hear someday, or perhaps you have already heard. Imagine that you are with someone, and these opinions are expressed. In the space provided, answer whether you would want to be involved in a conversation with a person who had uttered each of these opinions: "yes," to indicate that you would want to keep talking, "no," to indicate that you want to change the subject—or, perhaps, to be magically transported to some place far away from anyone who has made such a remark. (Hint: The opinions might seem random. But, there is a pattern underlying their sequence. See whether you can detect this pattern and what the pattern might mean.)

1. That new student is not a very nice person. _____
2. Boys are so stupid! _____
3. The teacher graded those essay tests unfairly! _____
4. The best athletes play soccer. _____
5. Basketball is a better sport than baseball. _____
6. Math is a more useful subject than history. _____

questions continued on the next page

DOI: 10.4324/9781003237150-36

7. Classical music is boring.   _____
8. Religious people are not fun to be around.   _____
9. Communism is bad; look what happened to the U.S.S.R.   _____
10. I think philosophy is very interesting!   _____

Take a minute or two and review the 10 opinions. Can you see the pattern? The sequence moves from an individual person through groups of people to subjects in school to forms of human activity. Then, the "best" opinion is saved until last, since philosophy is interested in all of the first nine opinions, and lots more of them besides!

If you put a "yes" after all 10 opinions, then it seems safe to say that you are interested in many things, from individual people to subjects as vast and important as art, religion, and philosophy. And, even if you entered "yes" after only a few of the opinions, you nonetheless indicated interest, and you would surely want to be involved in conversations during which these opinions were discussed, or to read about or in some way experience the subjects mentioned in these opinions. After all, many of the opinions are controversial—not to mention that some of them are, perhaps, a bit on the silly side.

The point is that, if you were in a conversation that revolved around any one of these opinions, you would probably learn something about the subject of these opinions and also about yourself as you expressed your beliefs and developed your ideas on these subjects.

"It is the disease of not listening . . . that I am troubled withal."
William Shakespeare, poet and playwright

For Further Thought

1. Think for a minute or so and then list the top five things or activities that you find boring beyond belief. After you have finished this list, ask yourself this question—and be honest: Exactly why do you find each of these things so boring? Are your reasons good, or have you merely not taken the time to investigate whatever it is that you currently find boring?

2. Do the same thing as described in 1, but then compare your list with that of a friend (or classmate) who has also done the list. Take turns giving reasons to explain why you are not interested in these activities and then see whether you and your friend can spot errors in the reasons given. This is good critical thinking, and you might be surprised by what happens!

Question #33

Should you criticize people or the opinions people have?

Occasionally, when we are talking with someone, we might think that something said is false, misleading, irrelevant, or vague. Should we comment on the point that is bothering us? If so, how should we do it?

Being clear about what we are hearing or reading or discussing is important (see **Question #31**), but it is not always easy to know how to improve the clarity of what other people are saying or writing. And it is also not always easy to know how to react to something people say that strikes us in a negative manner.

Here are three examples of responses someone might make to a claim or assertion by another person. Read them carefully and then be ready to take a short quiz about these responses:

1. *Mary*:   Too many movies these days contain excessive violence.
   Bill: Just what you'd expect a girl to say about action films.

2. *Adolf*:   Democracy is the best form of government.
   Josef: How could you, as an American citizen, have any other opinion?

3. *Jenny*:   In philosophy class, we studied how Thomas Aquinas proved the existence of God. I thought it made a lot of sense.
   Jill: Aquinas was Catholic, wasn't he? I wouldn't take what he said about God seriously if I were you.

Here is the quiz. Answer "yes" or "no" to the following questions:

1. Does Bill show that Mary's point about movies having excessive violence is incorrect just because he has indicated that she, the speaker of this proposition, is a girl?

      Yes _____ No _____

questions continued on the next page

DOI: 10.4324/9781003237150-37

2. Is Adolf's point about democracy being the best form of government *refuted*—that is, shown to be false—when Josef indicates that Adolf, the speaker of this proposition, is himself an American?

    Yes _____ No _____

3. Has Jill shown that Aquinas' proof for the existence of God is false—whatever that proof might be—just by indicating to Jenny that Aquinas was Catholic?

    Yes _____ No _____

If you answered "no" to all three questions, then you have the ability to distinguish between *what* a person is saying and *who* the person is saying it. If you answered "yes" to one, some, or all of the three questions, then you have been guilty of the logical fallacy called "*attacking the person.*" Look again at each of the three examples:

1. Ask yourself: Could a boy make the same claim as Mary? Of course. Would you argue that the claim was correct just because a *boy* were to say it? Of course not. So, does it matter whether the speaker of the claim is a boy or a girl? Whether or not some movies have excessive violence is an opinion that may or may not be true. But its truth or falsity will not be determined by looking at the gender of the person making the claim. We will have to examine the movies in question—not Mary—in order to decide whether or not Mary's opinion is true or false.

2. Must all American citizens necessarily believe that democracy is the best form of government? No. You could be an American citizen and still question whether the country should be under another form of government.

    Indeed, philosophers have been discussing the best form of government for 3,000 years. Nowadays, an American citizen might honestly think that democracy is the best form of government. Indeed, the vast majority of American citizens probably do share this conviction. But if that opinion about government is true, it is because of the nature of democracy itself, not just because someone living as a citizen under a democracy claims that it is the best type of government. Whether or not Adolf himself is an American does not matter to the point Adolf is making about the best form of government.

3. The third example is a bit more subtle than the first two. Jill is not attacking Jenny directly; rather, she is indicating a feature about the person—

Aquinas—who has said something of which Jenny approves. Since Aquinas was indeed Catholic, then, according to Jill, this means that Jenny should not accept Aquinas' reasoning about the existence of God.

Whether or not Aquinas' proof for the existence of God (see **Question #26**) is valid does not depend on Aquinas' religious beliefs. If Aquinas has made a mistake in this proof, he made it not because he is Catholic, but because his ability as a philosopher somehow failed him. Catholic philosophers and non-Catholic philosophers reason in exactly the same way. If Aquinas' proof is not persuasive, the problem lies in the proof itself, not in the fact that Aquinas, the author of the proof, was Catholic.

The main point here is that, when we want to evaluate something a person says (or writes), we should concentrate on *what is said*, not on *who is saying it*. Since we are speaking with—or, perhaps, arguing with—another human being, we tend to be overly impressed with the fact that a flesh-and-blood person is in our midst. But it is essential for good critical thinking to separate *what is being said* from *who is saying it*. In this way, we will be in a position to assess the truth and value of the point under discussion, rather than merely utter irrelevant comments about the person partaking in the discussion. In philosophy, opinions and positions are evaluated, not people.

For Further Thought

1. How common is the logical fallacy of attacking the person? Can you recall an occasion when you might have been guilty of this fallacy? If so, can you reproduce the situation and now attempt a more relevant critical argument against the position held by this person?

2. Although avoiding logical fallacies is usually an important feature in good reasoning, there are times when what would be a fallacy under normal circumstances becomes prudent strategy. Can you think of situations when it might be justified (a) to attack the person rather than (b) to attack what the person said?

"I love criticism just so long as it's unqualified praise."
Noel Coward, playwright

Question #34

Why is "because" such an important word?

*"The gods plant reason in mankind,
of all good gifts the highest."*
Sophocles, poet and playwright

"Just because!" Have you ever heard someone (a parent or, perhaps, a teacher) answer a question with *"Just because"*? If so, did this response answer your question? *"Just because"* might have stopped you from asking any more questions—at least for now—but, it is hardly an effective and satisfying reply for any question that was seriously asked.

Why do we answer questions with *"Just because"*? Perhaps it is because we are tired, or uninterested in the question, or irritated with the person asking the question. Many explanations are possible, and they concern situations that people—all people—often face in their daily lives.

But if we are serious about a question, then we must be serious about its answer. The following activity is based on a particular question that you may have already thought about on your own.

John to Mary: *"I am an intelligent person!"*
Mary to John: *"How do you know?"*

Imagine that John (or, of course, anyone) gave the following reasons to explain the belief that he is intelligent. Rank the reasons according to how well each explains John's claim. Use a scale from 1 to 4 ranked as follows:

1 = Good thinking!
2 = An adequate reason.
3 = Are you sure that makes sense?
4 = Sorry, forget it!

DOI: 10.4324/9781003237150-38

a. Because I am human.   _____

b. Because I am smart.   _____

c. Because I like to read books.   _____

d. Because my parents are intelligent   _____

e. Because I've always been intelligent.   _____

f. Because my vocabulary is excellent.   _____

g. Because I get the highest grades in school.   _____

h. Because I do very well on standardized exams.   _____

i. Because all my close friends are intelligent.   _____

j. Because I like to do the activities in *Philosophy for Kids*.   _____

k. Because I enjoy all the subjects we study at school.   _____

l. Because I am good at many different things.   _____

For Further Thought

1. Do this ranking activity with a friend and then compare the results. Group your responses, that is, list all the answers for which you both gave 1, 2, and so forth. Discuss and critically evaluate why you ranked the reasons as you did.

2. Is any reason to which you assigned a 1 adequate *by itself* to explain intelligence? If not, is it necessary to *combine* reasons in order to give a better explanation? Could more than one reason be worth ranking as 1?

3. This activity shows that, whenever we say "because" in order to explain something—especially a concept as complicated as intelligence—we must try to keep in mind that giving an adequate explanation is often complex, with many different aspects and phases.

4. The 12 reasons given in the activity are intended to answer how someone *knows* that a certain proposition is true. For a discussion of what, in general, it means to have knowledge, see **Question #16**.

"My reason is not framed to bend or stoop;
my knees are."
Michel de Montaigne, essayist

Question #35

Is it always easy to tell what causes things to happen?

"I know that you did it."
"How do you know?"
"Because you were there just before it happened!"

If you were watching a mystery show on television and you heard two characters have the above conversation, what would you think of this reasoning? Not very good, eh? But why? The answer seems simple: Just because a person was at a place before something happened there, it cannot be certain that this person caused whatever it was that happened.

This kind of thinking can be—and, unfortunately, is—also used in many other contexts. Read the following list of explanations and see whether you can detect a pattern common to all of them:

1. My grades went down this year. I hope I get easier teachers next year.
2. Mary has a cold—I told her she was not dressing warmly enough.
3. This man paid what he owed with crisp, new $20 bills. He must have been the bank robber we just heard about on the news!
4. The death penalty in the U. S. has resulted in a very high crime rate.
5. Since the Federal Government became active in public education, we now have the highest number of people who cannot read in the industrialized world.
6. The experiment didn't work; I must not have mixed the chemicals in the correct proportion.
7. William has difficulty making friends, no doubt because his home life has not been especially happy.
8. We lost. I knew the coach gave us the wrong game plan!
9. Jan lost the election; she did not spend enough money on campaign advertising.

DOI: 10.4324/9781003237150-39

The pattern found in all the examples is, simply stated, that "X causes Y," that there is a causal connection between one event or thing and another event or thing. But, is the evidence in each example adequate to establish that connection? If the evidence is *not* adequate, then the speaker has been guilty of the fallacy of "*questionable cause.*"

For example, in 1, it is certainly possible that your grades went down this semester because the teachers you had were strict and hard graders. But, there could be a number of other explanations (e.g., that you spent too much time watching television or playing computer games). So if you wanted to explain the cause of your lower grades, you would also have to consider these other possibilities before you drew a causal conclusion.

Whenever we say that something "causes" something else, we are establishing a connection between two things or events. Sometimes, this connection is easily seen and would never be questioned. If you go for a brisk walk when the temperature outside is 100 degrees, it is safe to say that your perspiration is caused by your body's reaction to the heat. But, if, for example, you are feeling a bit tense, it is not always easy to determine what "causes" that feeling.

It is important that we be aware of the importance—and the complexity—of the concept of "cause." In everyday life, we often do not have time to reflect on what or how something causes something else. But, this lack of attention to cause and effect normally does not harm us or interfere with attaining the goals we are pursuing. We should, nonetheless, be careful when we say that something causes something else unless we are fairly certain that there is indeed a causal "link" between the two "somethings." We do not want to assert that there are causal connections in the world when, in fact, they do not exist!

For Further Thought

1. The above examples illustrating the fallacy of questionable cause cover a wide range of activities: education, government, athletics, science, religion, ordinary life, to name a few. In which type of activity is it easiest to determine accurately causes that are true?

    On the next page, rank the following six activities, using 1 for the activity or area in which the highest degree of causal certainty can, in general, be found, 2 for the second highest degree, and so forth:

science _____
religion _____
philosophy _____
politics _____
athletics _____
ordinary life _____

2. What reasons made you rank these activities as you did? Why do you think that any one of these activities is more or less certain than any of the others? This question focuses on the concept of *causality*. This important concept has been analyzed and explained by a number of philosophers. For one of the most interesting—and challenging—treatments of causality and how it relates to the "laws" of science, see **Question #15**.

3. If you want to test yourself to see how well you have understood this activity, take any—or all—of the nine examples given and identify the (assumed) causes, then evaluate them. If the causes are weak, explain why they are weak. You will discover that this kind of critical thinking is interesting, and informative—and enjoyable!

*"Some play at chess, some at cards, some at the
Stock Exchange. I prefer to play at Cause and Effect."*
Ralph Waldo Emerson, essayist and poet

Question #36

If many people believe that something is true, is it true?

"We are all of us, more or less, the slaves of opinion."
William Hazlitt, essayist and painter

"The earth is flat. Everyone knows that!" If this statement were made in Europe around the year 1450 (or earlier), it is almost certain that everyone would have agreed. After all, the earth *was* flat! Or so most people believed.

Today, we know that the earth is spherical, not flat. If someone now said *"The earth is flat,"* he or she would be looked at very strangely. People would wonder whether this individual was joking or trying to achieve some sort of theatrical effect. Of course, the earth was spherical in 1450 as well as now. So, the fact that in 1450 almost everyone *believed* that the earth was flat meant nothing about the shape of the earth. But it did mean something about this particular belief: It was incorrect, pure and simple.

Just because many people believe that something is true, it is not necessary that what they believe really *is* true. Almost everyone nowadays believes that the earth is spherical. But, the proposition "The earth is spherical" is not true because most people believe it to be true. "The earth is spherical" is true because . . . well, the earth *is* spherical and can be proven by observation to be so. Whether or not people choose to believe this fact is irrelevant to its being true. (See **Question #12** for a famous philosopher's theory of truth.)

It is a logical fallacy to conclude that something must be true *simply because* most people believe it to be true. People differ in the beliefs that they accept as true. In the space provided on the next page, write whether you think the following beliefs would be accepted by "none," "some," "many," or "all" the people

111

DOI: 10.4324/9781003237150-40

who knew and cared about the content of these beliefs.

1. Michael Jordan was the best basketball player ever.   _____
2. The planet Mars once supported humanoid life forms.   _____
3. Men do not often express their emotions.   _____
4. Smoking cigarettes is O.K.   _____
5. Practice makes perfect.   _____
6. Goodness will triumph over evil.   _____
7. There is a life after death.   _____
8. God exists.   _____

For Further Thought

1. Your answers for the eight opinions probably vary, depending on the opinion. Why? Does the explanation depend on (a) what the opinion says or (b) people's reaction to the opinion? Ask your friends or classmates to do this activity and then compare and discuss the results.

2. Is it possible for people to *make* an opinion true by believing in it? For example, if everyone on earth believed that there was once life on Mars, would that universal belief make life exist on Mars? Of course not. But what if everyone on earth believed that "practice makes perfect"? If everyone believed that practice makes perfect, would everyone become perfect at whatever they did as long as they practiced it over and over?

3. If you are wondering about the difference between belief and knowledge, see **Question #16** for a discussion of this important distinction in epistemology.

*"Opinion is ultimately determined
by the feelings, and not by the intellect."*
Herbert Spencer, philosopher

Question #37

Do two wrongs balance out and make an action right?

Sometimes we do things we shouldn't. Sometimes we're *caught* doing things we shouldn't. When this happens, it is natural to try to defend ourselves, especially when the person who catches us is a parent or teacher.

Mounting a defense in these kinds of situations takes thought. But, some thought is more effective than other thought. And when the situation involves actions that are inappropriate, then thinking clearly when we are in the midst of trying to establish a defense is very difficult to do. Our emotions are running wild. What, we ask ourselves, can be done to get out of this trouble?

Consider the following situation: John is taking a test. He glances across the aisle and sees Bill cheating (Bill is looking at Mary's paper for an answer). John thinks to himself, "*If Bill can cheat, so can I.*" The teacher catches John cheating and, after class, decrees his punishment. John's defense to the teacher: "*You can't just punish me—Bill was cheating too!*"

Have you ever tried to defend yourself as John has just done? You may never have cheated on a test, but if you ever did something you shouldn't have, then you might have tried to get yourself out of the situation by pointing to someone else who had done the same thing. How successful is this kind of defense?

Let's consider a series of examples that resemble the sample situation described above. Look carefully at each situation, then answer the question "yes" or "no." Try to be as honest as possible when you answer.

(Hint: There is a pattern underlying the sequence of five situations. See whether you can detect it, then see whether you can figure out what the pattern might be suggesting.)

1. If someone insults you, it is okay for you to insult them back.

   Yes _____   No _____

questions continued on the next page

DOI: 10.4324/9781003237150-41

2. If someone becomes angry at you and then hits you, it is okay for you to become angry at that person and hit him or her back.

    Yes _____ No _____

3. If someone steals something from you, it is okay for you to steal something from that person.

    Yes _____ No _____

4. If some adults cheat the government on their tax returns, it is okay for you as an adult to cheat the government on your tax returns.

    Yes _____ No _____

5. If one nation steals defense secrets from another nation, it is okay for the second nation to steal defense secrets from the first nation.

    Yes _____ No _____

The principle "*two wrongs don't make a right*" is well known. It is used to refute a person trying to justify a wrong action when he or she has been subjected to a similar wrong action. But, is this principle *always* true? Is it possible that, in some cases, two wrongs *do* make a right?

For Further Thought

1. Answering 1 and 2 above with "no" is easy. But would it be easy to *do* what you were supposed to do? If someone insults us or hits us in anger, it is very difficult not to do the same thing in return. But, even if we did do the same thing back, would it be right? If it is wrong to insult someone or to hit him or her in anger, is it right to do these actions to someone after he or she has done those actions to you? Surely the answer is "no."

2. In the third example, we must *decide* to steal something. But, if stealing is wrong, then is it right to steal something from someone who has stolen something from you? If stealing is stealing, then the circumstances in this case would not seem to matter. If someone steals something from you, it is wrong for you to steal something from him or her in return.

3. The fourth example requires *careful* thought. If you cheat the government at tax time, you must do so in a way guaranteeing—you hope—that you don't get caught. But, does the fact that many people act in this way make it right for you to do the same thing? Surely not.

4. The fifth example involves one government acting toward another government. In this case, the original theft has been authorized by an official government agency. But, does this factor matter as far as determining the rightness of the action by the second government?

   The pattern in the five examples moves from emotional situations to reasoned situations to a situation involving reasoned decisions by officials governing a nation. Does the principle "*two wrongs don't make a right*" apply in *all* cases? For instance, in the fifth example, does the fact that defense secrets might be essential in protecting a nation mean that this principle no longer applies? Is the second nation justified in stealing defense secrets from the first nation in order to preserve its citizens *as* a nation?

   If you are hesitating, then perhaps "*two wrongs don't make a right*" as a principle is not *always* correct! Think about the circumstances of the fifth example, then try to explain why you think the principle does—or does not—apply in this case. If you decide that the principle does not apply in this example, perhaps it might not also apply to some of the earlier examples.

   Thinking these examples through provides good practice in applying a general principle to particular cases, a procedure that philosophers must do almost all the time (See **Question #1**). "*Two wrongs don't make a right*" surely applies in many cases. But, does it apply in *all* cases?

"*Wrongs do not leave off there
where they begin,
But still beget new mischiefs
in their course.*"
Samuel Daniel, poet and historian

Question #38

"I am lying."
True or false?

Here is the simplest true/false examination you will ever take:

1. The moon is made of green cheese.   True _____   False _____

2. Some apples are red.   True _____   False _____

This challenging quiz illustrates the fact that logic generally assumes that propositions are either true or false. Of course, not all propositions are true or false. For example, the proposition "*It will rain tomorrow*" is, strictly speaking, neither true nor false since it is about the future and the future is unknown. But, logic, at least at an elementary level, operates by assuming that many of the propositions we ordinarily speak are either true or false. (Oh, yes, just in case: 1 is false, 2 is true.)

However, there are simple propositions that behave quite oddly as far as truth and falsity are concerned. Some of these propositions are philosophically interesting and important. Consider the proposition "*I am lying.*" Let's continue with the true/false examination:

3. I am lying.   True _____   False _____

Notice what happens: If "I am lying" is true, then it is false to say that I have told a lie since I said I was lying; but, if "I am lying" is false, then I have told the truth when I said I was lying. So, if "I am lying" is true, then it is false, and if "I am lying" is false, then it is true.

What's Happening Here?

Perplexed? Don't be. We have just witnessed the "Liar Paradox," a phenomenon discovered by an unknown Greek logician in the 4th century B.C. A *paradox* is something puzzling and difficult to comprehend. The paradox here refers

DOI: 10.4324/9781003237150-42

to one sentence that produces contradictory conclusions. Such a sentence is *extremely* puzzling and difficult to comprehend.

One way to gain insight into the Liar Paradox is to think about the title of a book by logician Raymond Smullyan containing many logic puzzles and problems. The name of this book is *What is the Name of this Book?*

Here is a skit, which you can perform with a friend or classmate, that dramatically shows the relevance of this title to the Liar Paradox. You need one prop: Print the sentence "What is the name of this book?" on a sheet of paper, cut it out, and tape it carefully to the front cover of a book (any book will do). Or, you can get a copy of Professor Smullyan's book! (See *Additional Readings in Philosophy* at the end of *Philosophy for Kids*.)

Scene:	a classroom
Cast:	a nameless teacher, Bertrand (a student)

Teacher: [holding up the book with the title page facing the class] Class, what is the name of this book?

Bertrand: [raising his hand eagerly] What is the name of this book?!

Teacher: Yes, Bertrand, that's the question.

Bertrand: And that's the answer!

Teacher: What answer?

Bertrand: What is the name of this book?

Teacher: That's *my* question!

Bertrand: And that's *my* answer!!

Teacher: What answer?

Bertrand: What is the name of this book?

Teacher: Yes.

Bertrand: Yes what?

Teacher: What is the name of this book?

Bertrand: I just told you!

Teacher: Told me what?

Bertrand: The answer to your question.

Teacher: What is the name of this book?

Bertrand: Right!

Teacher: [turning toward the blackboard and muttering] Good grief, students don't seem to be as bright as they used to be.

Bertrand: [sinking in his seat and muttering] Golly, teachers don't seem to be as bright as they used to be.

For Further Thought

1. Can you see what caused all the confusion? (Hint: Think about what words do whenever someone tells a lie. If I say "*I did not take the cookie*" when I did take the cookie, then I have lied. Now look at "*I did not take the cookie.*" To what does this proposition refer, or point to? It refers to an action—taking the cookie—that I deny having done. So, if we tell a lie, we use a proposition to refer to a certain kind of action.

   Now look at "*I am lying.*" What do those words refer to? Aha! The proposition "*I am lying*" refers to *itself*! However, the proposition "*I did not take the cookie from the jar*" refers to something *other* than itself, that is, to a certain action. Here is the source of the paradox. Philosophers—who like to make up big words—have a name for a proposition such as "*I am lying.*" They call it "*self-referential,*" meaning that the proposition refers to itself. There are many examples of self-referential propositions (many of them humorous). Perhaps you can think of some to illustrate this concept.

2. One way to resolve the Liar Paradox is to recognize the difference between what propositions *mean* and what they *refer to*. We now realize that, before we can tell whether a proposition is true or false, we must be clear about (a) what the proposition refers to and (b) what the proposition means. The Liar Paradox reveals, in dramatic (and perhaps amusing) fashion, the importance of this distinction. By the way, the study of language is a prominent area in contemporary philosophy. Speaking is one of the most fascinating things human beings do!

3. The distinction between *meaning* and *referencing* is very important in philosophy. For another discussion of a situation that is almost as paradoxical as the Liar Paradox, see **Question #11**.

4. Lies are usually directed toward other people. But, is it possible for you to lie to yourself? See **Question #18** for the French philosopher Jean-Paul Sartre's thoughts on this intriguing question.

"[They] who cannot lie do not know what the truth is."
Friedrich Nietzsche, philosopher

Question #39

Can something logical ever not make sense?

"You're not being logical!"
"Yes I am!"

Does this exchange sound familiar? Have you ever accused someone, or been accused yourself, of not being logical?

Ask yourself whether you are a logical person. Most people would say "yes." But, how do you know that you are logical? In fact, just what does it *mean* to be logical? Here is a multiple-choice question that will reveal something about whether you are logical in a philosophical sense:

1. *If it is true that*—(A): all horses are four-legged animals
   and
   if it is true that—(B): all four-legged animals have feet,

then which one of these four propositions can be stated if propositions A and B are combined—or, in short, if we *reason* with A and B?

   a. All animals are horses.
   b. All animals have four legs.
   c. All horses have feet.
   d. No things with feet have four legs.

Did you answer c? If you did, then you are logical. If propositions A and B are combined, then logically they imply proposition c. But, can you explain why this combination of proposition produces such a logical result? If you cannot tell why, then you are a logical person—but only sort of. This means that you can recognize when something is logical but, at the moment anyway, you are not absolutely clear as to why it *must* be this way. So, the next time you are asked to be logical, you might not be!

DOI: 10.4324/9781003237150-43

119

Let's try another question; perhaps the answer will help explain why logic is logical. (This question is a bit trickier, so you will have to concentrate in order to figure out the answer.)

2. If (C) all houses are antelopes
   and
   if (D) all antelopes are funny

then which of the following four propositions can be said if we reason by combining propositions C and D?

   e. All antelopes are houses.
   f. All houses are funny.
   g. All funny houses are expensive.
   h. Houses cannot be antelopes and antelopes cannot be funny—so Example 2 simply cannot be logical!

Question #39 asks "*Can something logical ever not make sense*"? Look at propositions C and D. Are they true or false? It is false to say that all houses are antelopes (it is more than false—it is very strange,) and to say that all antelopes are funny is also false (and also very strange). But, the question is whether anything *logical* happens when C and D are combined, even if these two propositions make no sense by themselves. The answer: Yes, something logical does happen. But, what?

What's missing if you compare Example 2 with Example 1? In Example 1, the phrase "If it is true that. . . ." appears *before* propositions A and B. This phrase is important in logic. Can you see why?

Let's return to Example 2. It is not true that "*all houses are antelopes*," nor is it true that "*all antelopes are funny.*" But—and here is the crucial point—if it were true that "*all houses are antelopes*" and if it were true that "*all antelopes are funny,*" then what would follow? It would follow that "*all houses are funny.*" So, if you selected answer f to Example 2, you are definitely logical. And, if you did not select answer (f), can you understand why (f) makes sense? If you assume that (C) and (D) are true, then (f) follows as true if we reason by combining (C) and (D). We can also see that the answer to **Question #39** is "yes." Something can indeed be logical and not make sense. It makes little sense to say that "*all houses are funny,*" but it would make sense to assert this statement *if* propositions (C) and (D) were true.

What is the reason for this rather unusual conclusion? In a way, you are still not *really* logical if you ask yourself why you chose (f) and you can't explain your choice. Let's see whether we can do something about that.

Here is a third multiple-choice question (circle the correct answer):

3. What is identical in propositions (A)–(B) and in propositions (C)–(D)?

   a. Nothing. (A) and (B) are about animals, horses, and legs; (C) and (D) are about houses, antelopes, and funniness.
   b. The two sets of propositions, (A)–(B) and (C)–(D), have the same *pattern*, or formal structure.
   c. Both sets of propositions are the type of things teachers say in school.
   d. Only a philosopher would think of propositions like these!

Answers c and d are not serious possibilities. However, you might have chosen a. If so, then look again at the *form* of the two sets of propositions. If you do, you recognize that the answer is b: The two sets of propositions do indeed have the same pattern, or formal structure.

Let's abbreviate the main elements in these two sets of propositions:

Example 1	**Example 2**
Horses = H	Houses = H
Four-legged animals = A	Antelopes = A
Feet = F	Funny = F

The first example of reasoning then becomes:

All H are A.
All A are F.
So, All H are F.

But, notice that the second example of reasoning also becomes:

All H are A.
All A are F.
So, all H are F.

The arrangement of the letters H, A, and F helps show what is happening in these two examples of reasoning. The examples have the same logical form because they both connect classes of things in exactly the same way. It does not matter to the logic of the reasoning that Example 2 contains propositions which are either false or silly—for *if* Example 1 is logical reasoning, then so is Example 2 because the classes in its three propositions are connected in exactly the same way as the classes in Example 1.

A *class* may be defined as a group of things sharing one or several characteristics. For example, houses come in many shapes and can be made of many different types of material, but if a house is understood as a place where people live, then all such buildings form the class of houses.

When we reason, we frequently reason with classes in mind: horses, houses, four-leggedness, antelopes, jokes, and so forth. And, if we reason according to certain formal arrangements of classes, then we reason correctly. This explains why the example of reasoning that connects houses and antelopes and being funny can produce a "logical" conclusion, even though the conclusion—"*All houses are funny*"—does not make sense by itself. So, we see then that something can be logical and not make sense after all!

Philosophers have named this feature of reasoning *validity*. So, Example 2 is valid reasoning. The form of its reasoning is correct, even though no one—not even a philosopher—normally talks about funny houses and antelopes that might really be houses in disguise.

For Further Thought

1. What is the difference between reasoning that is valid and reasoning that concludes by saying something true? (Hint: Compare the propositions in Example 1 with those in Example 2. How do they differ?)

2. Which is more important—valid reasoning or saying things that are true? (See **Question #12** for a discussion of what it means in philosophy to say something that is true.)

3. Can you think of an example of reasoning that is not valid because of the way the classes are arranged and combined in the propositions?

4. The arguments in Examples 1 and 2 both contain three propositions, the third proposition in each case being a *conclusion* drawn from the first two propositions (called *premises*). Are at least two propositions *always* needed in order to reason?

"'Contrariwise,' continued Tweedledee, 'if it was so,it might be;
and if it were so, it would be: but as it isn't, it ain't. That's logic."
Lewis Carroll, author and logician

Question #40

"I wonder . . ." what it means to define something?

*"If you wish to converse with me,
define your terms."*
Voltaire, author and philosopher

All of us have been in conversations—or arguments—where someone involved has made a comment similar to Voltaire's. Whenever this happens, discussion tends to halt, at least until the person challenged hunts for some suitable phrase to define a term, usually a complex term (otherwise its meaning would not be in dispute). We need a definition!

But, "*What is a definition?*" is itself a very important question in philosophy. We do different things when we explain our terms, and many of these functions have been called "definitions." It is important, therefore, to be aware of these differences.

Below are two exercises: The first exercise is easy; in the second, you can demonstrate your ability to think philosophically about definitions.

Match the terms with their definitions by writing the term next to its correct definition in the space provided.

  (a) centaur   (b) heat   (c) capitalism   (d) black hole

1. Gravitationally completely collapsed star. _____
2. A mythical beast with the body of a horse
   and the head of a man. _____
3. A form of energy possessed by a body due to
   the irregular motion of its molecules. _____
4. Freedom in the economic sphere. _____

Obviously, you could have looked up each of these four terms in the dictionary. In that respect, all these definitions are "dictionary definitions." But, if

DOI: 10.4324/9781003237150-44

you examine the four definitions more carefully, you will notice that there are important differences among them. The dictionary is not very helpful for determining these differences—but philosophy is!

Here are brief descriptions of four frequently used kinds of definition:

Stipulative: proposing to use a term in a certain way, usually new (e.g., using "googol" to define "the number 10 raised to the power 100").

Lexical: the dictionary, or "lexic,"—from the Greek *legein*, "to say or speak"—meaning of a term that already has an established usage (e.g., "house" defined as "a structure serving as a dwelling for one or more persons, especially for a family").

Theoretical: stating the meaning of a term so that it can function as part of a scientific or philosophical explanation (e.g., "class" defined as a characteristic or characteristics common to a group of beings).

Persuasive: using language in order to persuade an audience that the stated terms adequately represent the word to be defined (e.g., "democracy" defined as "the most free form of government by the people").

Now, for a truly philosophical exercise! The definitions given on page 121 are numbered 1 through 4. Listed below are the names of the four *types* of definition just outlined. See whether you can identify what type of definition is represented by the definitions given in 1 through 4 above. In the space provided below, write the *number* of the definition next to its corresponding *type*. If you can do this exercise, then you have shown the ability to distinguish and identify examples of different types of definition.

Stipulative   _____
Lexical   _____
Theoretical   _____
Persuasive   _____

For Further Thought

1. Distinguishing types of definitions is often a subtle and complex exercise. However, the more skill you possess in identifying the ways in which a term is defined, the greater is your ability to think critically about how these terms are used in arguments and discussions.

2. It is a common belief that the dictionary provides the final word on questions of definitions. "*Look it up!*" is a cry often heard when a dispute arises about the meaning of a word. However, what kind of definition would the dictionary provide for a concept such as "justice" or "time"? And, more importantly, would this definition help resolve any philosophical disagreement that might arise about the meaning of that concept? Dictionaries are extremely useful tools, but they have limits when it comes to certain types of concept. When these limits are reached, only a philosopher can help!

"[They] shall be a god to me, who can rightly divide and define."
Ralph Waldo Emerson, essayist and poet

A Further—and Final— Thought

You are now at the conclusion of *Philosophy for Kids*. The final chapter has presented an opportunity to practice some of the important aspects in the art of defining terms. In fact, all the chapters in the Critical Thinking Part IV section of this book have helped you prepare not only for more philosophy, but for a clearer understanding of everything you read and discuss with other people.

Philosophers spend a great deal of time and energy thinking about definitions. But, philosophers also think about what conclusions they can reason to, given the definitions that have been accepted. It is essential to have the most secure definitions possible. But, it is even more essential that a philosopher—and you—be willing to *think* about the issues and problems that have been the subject of the 40 questions in this book.

If you have found the experience of thinking through the chapters in *Philosophy for Kids* to be enjoyable and informative, then you might want to glance at the section *Additional Reading in Philosophy,* which begins on p. 182. There, you'll discover other books that will provide additional challenges in philosophy from a number of different perspectives and in a variety of styles.

Long ago, the Greek philosopher Socrates said that the unexamined life is not worth living. *Philosophy for Kids* has helped you to start examining your life along avenues that philosophers have opened for our thoughtful consideration. Such examination is important, essential, and also thoroughly enjoyable. For all readers of *Philosophy for Kids*, however, the *real* fun is just beginning!

How To Philosophize
if You Are Not
a Philosopher

*I*f you have not thought of yourself as a philosopher, or even as philosophically inclined, you may be surprised to learn *everyone* is a philosopher, at least to a certain degree.

Every time you decide that something is in your "best interests" or is "for the best," you are being philosophical. Identifying your interests means being able to discriminate between what concerns you and what you can safely ignore, this amidst the limitless welter of the world's business. Once this is accomplished, you review what is "best" for you, at least as you currently see things. This determination is a fundamental exercise in ethics, i.e., in determining value and how it affects the practical dimensions of your life. This sense of value is resolved and activated within a varied and complex context—yourself as an individual human being, your family, friends, associates, your home, city, country—in short, your world. Each concrete or "practical" decision you make resonates throughout this ensemble of environments.

From another perspective, various aspects of you as a "knowing" individual (that is, what you sense, perceive, understand) must come into play in order for you to assimilate all the data that come streaming into your world and select those elements that will ground and inform your subsequent decisions.

And finally, these decisions are based on a set of assumptions concerning what constitutes, for you, the nature of reality and what might appear real until it is considered critically and is then recognized as something only apparently real and without substantial value to your interests. For example, how "real" is what other people think of you? Is this an essential dimension of reality as far as you are concerned, or do you dismiss their opinions as irrelevant? The answer to this question determines, in part, the reality of your world as far as attitudes, thoughts, and decisions are concerned.

Making decisions based on values, knowing what is going on around you, dealing with reality in a clear and logical way—this is the "stuff" of everyday life. It is also precisely what philosophers think about. The only difference between a nonphilosopher and a philosopher is that the philosopher takes time to reflect on things and tries to institute order and system into the onrushing complexity of everyday life. Furthermore, the typical tools of the philosopher are common to all human beings: thoughts and words in the form of concepts, propositions, clarifications, explanations and reasoning.

No one should be intimidated by philosophy. When you read and think about things philosophically, you are thoughtfully interacting with all the fascinating—and vitally important—textures of life as it surrounds and penetrates us every day. Therefore, if philosophy is approached as an intellectual adventure of the highest order—which it is—then teachers and parents are in for a treat as they help guide, and also are guided by, the young people in their charge. Let's begin!

This chapter offers suggestions to teachers and parents for using *Philosophy for Kids*. The chapter is in four parts:

Organization: a detailed description of the basic structure of the book.

Classroom Procedures: general suggestions for presenting the book in class and, with suitable modifications, at home.

Question Review and Teaching Tips: A brief summary of the main theme of each question, followed by "Teaching Tips"—specific suggestions for presenting the activity and developing the content of each question.

Curricular Integration: a number of possibilities for integrating various questions in *Philosophy for Kids* with standard subjects for younger students.

Organization

Philosophy for Kids is divided into four sections. These sections—**Values**, **Knowledge**, **Reality**, **Critical Thinking**—represent four major areas in philosophy. The technical names for these areas are: **Ethics** (values), **Epistemology** (knowledge), **Metaphysics** (reality), **Logic** (critical thinking). Philosophy can be divided into additional areas and subtopics but these four domains are generally considered to be fundamental to the discipline.

A. **Order of Questions**. The four sections are arranged in this sequence based on an underlying principle of order. The sections move from the social or interactive immediacy of values to progressively more abstract concerns—questions pertaining to how we know and then to questions about what is real. This order tends to reflect the typical interests of younger students. They are frequently enmeshed in value questions ("*That's not fair!*" or "*Are you my friend?*"), hence the concepts of fairness and friendship open this section of the book. Questions pertaining to various areas in knowing occur in Part II since they are less immediately personal. Issues concerning the nature of reality follow in Part III, since they are, as a rule, the most abstract, but also, once discovered—and when the young person really begins to wonder—perhaps the most interesting of all. Finally, the critical thinking section in Part IV poses questions about clear and logical thinking. This section concludes the book since these discussions apply not only to each of the first three domains, but also to virtually any subject that students will study during their formal schooling.

B. **Sequence of Questions**. The questions in each of the first three parts are arranged according to the historical sequence of the philosophers serving as the primary focal point of each question, from the beginnings of philosophy up to the present day. Thus, the first three Parts begin with an ancient Greek philosopher. This principle of organization conveys, if only indirectly, the fact that philosophy has an essential historical dimension and, therefore, that later philosophers learn much from earlier philosophers.

Note that, if one were to do all 40 questions in sequence, the result would be a miniaturized introduction to philosophy course, following its historical progression and canvassing (in order) the areas of ethics, epistemology, metaphysics, and logic. Such a comprehensive approach is optional, of course. Teachers and parents are free to move about the book, exploring whatever questions mood and interest suggest.

C. **Internal Links**. Connections between and among the 40 questions appear frequently within each question—for example, the discussion of Aristotle's theory of friendship (**Question #2**) includes a reference to **Question #1**, which concerns Plato's approach to the virtue of justice. As noted in the Introduction, this interlocking effect reflects the fact that philosophy is an organic discipline. Thus, an interest in a specific issue can lead to various other issues seemingly unrelated to the point of the original inquiry. In philosophy, anything can lead to everything.

Classroom Procedures

A. **Preparation**: The point of the activities is not to establish a single conclusion—a "right" answer—but to present a range of possibilities that can collectively serve as fertile ground for discussion.

1. Read the question selected for class and familiarize yourself with its content and with the structure of the activity, reminding yourself to be ready for anything as far as questions from students are concerned.

2. The questions in this book were field-tested with students in grades 4–10. It was widely noted that the activities, in conjunction with the discussions, often engendered student response since these discussions are written in part to stimulate interest, as well as to explain. If this kind of response occurs, then the activities will become self-contained units in their own right. In general, if a spin-off discussion emerges concerning a point of merit and students are engaged, then it might be better, all things considered, to "go with the flow" and let this issue be the day's topic, rather than to abort thoughtful interchanges and refocus attention on the activity.

3. Note that the section **For Further Thought**, which concludes each question, contains questions and comments that could be used as means of producing discussion and further development of the main theme of that question.

B. **In the Classroom**: How teachers practice their art in the classroom is, of course, a highly personal matter. The following suggestions are only that, suggestions, not rules. However, they have served the author well over many years teaching philosophy, and they may prove useful here as a set of general guidelines for how the material in this book might be effectively presented.

1. *Use a concrete example to initiate discussion.* Keep in mind, however, that one must also try to avoid an extended anecdotal conversation based on the students' concrete examples. If this happens, the discussion will become a round-table series of first-person stories, interesting perhaps, but not an in-depth theoretical analysis of a given issue.

2. *Be open-minded.* You may personally have very strong convictions about the concept or issue that is the focal point of a particular question. But, try to suppress your own position in deference to whatever the students may produce in responding to the content of the question. Of course, you can always pose problems and ask questions that presuppose that your own position is correct, or at least that it is a reasonable possibility. But, if a student's response does not square with your expectations or beliefs, try not to say or even intimate that "*You're wrong!*" After all, the point of the discussion is not to provide a sounding board for the teacher's personal beliefs, but to allow the students to develop their own positions as fully and as coherently as possible. The teacher guides, rather than dictates, discussion.

3. In the same vein, *let the students do the talking as often as possible*, whether to you or to each other. If the teacher has a tendency to indulge in monologues, the students tend to expect the teacher to do all the talking, even when the teacher ceases to speak! Socrates almost never lectured; but, he did ask lots of questions and he always listened very carefully to the answers.

4. *Be flexible regarding the direction of discussion.* You may assume that children will react to a given question in a certain way. Sometimes, they will do exactly that. But, often they will not. Be prepared for young people to be creative in extending any one of the 40 questions into related—or unrelated—areas. Therefore, try not to be overly rigid if discussion of the questions begins to move beyond the apparent boundaries of the topic at hand. It is exciting to see young people generate their own questions and detect connections between the various topics explicitly introduced and discussed. Some practice may be necessary before being able to decide, on the spot, whether to redirect the conversation to the main theme of the question or to follow the side issue and see where it goes.

    In this regard, several teachers noted during field testing that the introductory discussion in the text leading to the activity often itself sparked questions and disputes. For example, the opening paragraph in **Question #2**, on Aristotle and friendship, asserts that anyone without friends would not only be lonely, but also not very happy. A group of fifth-grade students challenged that claim on the grounds that an individual ensconced with computer games would hardly need other people in order to enjoy life. Thus, students were already philosophizing about a point that the author believed (following Aristotle) was self-evident! Although the discussions leading to the activities are intended to be primarily explanatory, when they instigate comment and discussion from students, it is up to the teacher's discretion whether to allow this discussion to continue or to proceed to the activity.

5. *Admit you don't know all the answers.* This is very important. Never be afraid to say, "*I don't know*," or "*I'll have to think about that,*" if a young person has asked a question or made an observation for which the appropriate response in your mind is, in fact, "*I don't know*" or "*I'll have to think about that.*" The vigorous pursuit of philosophical questions often produces a state of confusion punctuated with a fervent desire for enlightenment—an occupational hazard, as it were, but an exhilarating one. An element of personal risk is involved whenever one participates in a free-wheeling philosophical discussion. However, the rewards of such discussion—greater understanding and wisdom concerning fundamental issues—far outweigh any potential drawbacks to preserving the elevated status of one's ego.

   In philosophy, no one has all the answers. Even if we believe we have the answers, they are doubtless only partial. As the eminent mathematician and philosopher Alfred North Whitehead put it, "All truths are only half-truths." It is a simple mark of honesty to admit that this lack of omniscience applies to you, as it does to everyone. Students will respect you all the more as a human being and as a fellow seeker after wisdom if such an admission occurs freely and without embarrassment. Just keep going!

Question Review and Teaching Tips

In this section, all 40 questions are briefly summarized, including the name of the philosopher and, where possible, the work of that philosopher on which the question is based. Each summary is then followed by a series of "Teaching Tips." These tips include:

1. suggestions for presenting each question;
2. typical student reactions that may be useful to know about in advance; and
3. supplementary remarks that may be instructive in discussing the philosophical content of each question with students.

The specific nature of the Teaching Tips varies from question to question, depending on the philosophical content and the type of activity. (Note also that there is no correlation between the numbering of the Teaching Tips listed below and the correspondingly numbered entries in the For Further Thought section of each question.)

Part I—Values

Question #1. Are you a fair and just person?
Plato (*Republic*)

Socrates critically assesses several attempts to define justice. This chapter also introduces the notion of defining and what it means to evaluate a definition.

Teaching Tips

1. The fact that the question asks what "should" be done in the various examples is important and should be emphasized. Socrates wants to know the answer to the moral question. He is not concerned to know what most people might, in fact, do in this situation. After all, what most people would actually do may, in the final analysis, not be the right thing to do.

2. After the students have done activity I, have them do activity II. Then, see whether they agree with the three comments on answers E, F, and H. Ask the students whether these answers are relevant, accurate, and fair. If there is disagreement, ask for their reasons.

3. As mentioned in the Introduction, the questions under **For Further Thought** (hereafter **FFT**) may be used for additional discussion and development of the concept under scrutiny, in this case justice. **FFT 1** is open-ended (i.e., there is no obvious answer, given what has been said about justice in the discussion). This question may be used to extend the students' appreciation for the importance of justice in relation to their friends. (This question also provides a link to **Question #2**, on friendship.)

4. The brief discussion in **FFT 3** of Plato's position in the *Republic* obviously gives only the barest indication of what Plato attempted to show about justice in this dialogue.

5. **FFT 2** and **3** can lead to an incisive discussion of being unjust to oneself (they also provide another natural link to the concept of duty, which is presented in **Question #4**). To initiate discussion, ask whether the students can think of an example of being unjust to themselves. Thus, does cheating on a test or plagiarizing an essay illustrate this kind of injustice?

6. Also of considerable interest is asking whether any student wants to attempt to define justice. Make clear that any such attempt will be carefully evaluated by other students who wish to emulate Socrates as a critical philosopher. Discussion will be intense and fruitful!

Question #2. How do you know who your friends are?
Aristotle (*Nicomachean Ethics*)

Aristotle presents a definition of friendship and description of three different types of friendship.

Teaching Tips

1. Before examining Aristotle's position, ask the students to define friendship on their own. They will undoubtedly assess each other's definitions—and do so critically—with great vigor. Let this discussion continue long enough to whet their philosophical appetites for an established definition (i.e., Aristotle's).

2. Before proceeding with Aristotle's definition, spend some time having the students discuss their reasons for or against the three types of friendship indicated in Examples A–C. This preliminary inquiry will sharpen their critical awareness when they begin to evaluate Aristotle's definition.

3. Aristotle argues that one type of friendship is based on utility, which young people tend to feel cannot be a legitimate form of friendship since, they claim, you are just "using" the other person. Note, however, that a friendship based on utility does satisfy all three requirements in Aristotle's definition of friendship. It is true that each party is "using" the other, but each party knows that he or she is being so used. Friendships based on utility do not include duplicity of any sort; if they did, this would violate the first condition of friendship, which is the reciprocal bearing of good will. In this case, one party would indeed be using the other party as a means to an end—clearly not friendship.

4. Regarding **FFT 3**: If some students claim that a percentage of their friendships are based on moral goodness, then the question becomes "*What is moral goodness?*" It would be prudent to assume that students will pose this question on their own. Aristotle spends a great deal of time on this concept in the *Nicomachean Ethics*, but his position may be summarized as "doing the right thing for the right reason." However, this slogan doubtless raises more questions than it solves. Thus, it is a fair response for the teacher to indicate that, in philosophy, not everything can be said at once. Although the question of moral goodness is important, it cannot be discussed here, when the immediate topic is friendship. For Aristotle, few friendships are based on moral virtue because there are few truly virtuous people (in, of course, his sense of virtue).

Question #3. Should you be rewarded for your efforts in school?
Confucius (*Analecta*)

In an aphorism, Confucius implies that effort is not nearly as important as results. The conflict between effort and results is very real to young people, especially in school settings. The exercises show how challenging it can be in an academic context to decide which is more important, effort or results.

Teaching Tips

1. The students will enjoy acting as teachers when they do the activity. Also, it will give them insight into the often-harrowing business of grading. Ask the students to give their results and put these results on the board (e.g., how many gave student #1 a D, a C, and so forth.). Then, ask for reasons to justify the grades assigned.

2. There is often considerable disagreement with the Confucianist position on effort. However, although modern students believe that effort should be rewarded, they are not always clear as to why this should be the case. If students claim that effort should be rewarded, ask for their reasons.

3. The three questions given in **FFT** usually arouse considerable interest. Gifted children are often the greatest defenders of students less academically able than they are; they do so by appealing to aspects of A, B, or C (or combinations thereof). It is fascinating to hear students talk about how they view their own intellectual abilities. The typical problem here will be in deciding the best way to close off discussion. If the content is good, consider extending the session on Confucius to a second day.

4. From a modern perspective, Confucius' extremely pragmatic position is difficult to defend. The point made at the end of **FFT 2** should be emphasized to the students in fairness to Confucius as a philosopher. Confucius' aphorisms are typically sensitive, kind, and gracious.

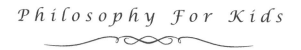

Question #4. Should you let little things bother you?
Marcus Aurelius (*Meditations*)

The Roman emperor emphasizes the importance of a stoical attitude about creature comforts and also the importance of doing one's duty.

Teaching Tips

1. Emphasize that the questions should be answered as honestly as possible. Also, not all questions may apply to each student. For example, some students might not like to watch sports; if so, then, for them, Question 7 is moot.

2. Where to draw the line exactly between a "little thing" and a "big thing" is not always easy. Discussing a criterion for this distinction is a good follow-up topic. How is one to decide between what is "little" (and, therefore, following Marcus Aurelius, something to be ignored) and something "big" (and, therefore, to be a subject of concern)?

3. Give the students a few minutes to produce duties to parents, teachers, friends, and themselves. Then, ask for examples of duties in each category and ask the class whether they would agree with each example given. The ensuing discussion will be rich—and contested!

Question #5. Is it your duty to give to charity?
Moses Maimonides

Maimonides argues that charity is a duty, his position depending on belief in God and in *The Bible* as the word of God. (But, can it be argued that we have duties to other human beings simply because we are all human?)

Teaching Tips

1. Emphasize that the answers to the activity should be as honest as possible (a range of answers will appear, regardless of class size). Describing students as "somewhat too self-centered" if they answer "no" rather than "yes" assumes that Maimonides' position on the duty of charity is correct. Students may dispute this characterization of their decision!

2. The **FFT** section separates questions 6 and 7 in the activity from questions 1–5. The students will readily identify Maimonides' two assumptions: (a) God exists and (b) Scripture is the revealed word of God. It may be noted to the students that, although most Americans might believe that (a) and (b) are true, this belief is not shared world-wide. (For a discussion of the existence of God, see **Question #26.**)

3. The discussion in **FFT 2** identifies the groups who are better off. The key philosophical question then becomes whether it would be a *duty* to help the poor, given this set of consequences. The point of this question is moral; that is, not *will* people help the poor but *should* people help the poor. Discussion of this point is often highly spirited. Some students believe that anyone on welfare is lazy and, therefore, giving charity to these people will be useless. Proponents of Maimonides would claim that even if this were true, it would still remain a duty to help the poor, regardless of whether or not some of them are lazy.

4. Asking the students to attempt to define duty in general (as opposed to a particular duty, such as being charitable) will provide a spirited—and controversial—way to conclude this question.

141

Question #6. Will having fun make you happier than studying?
John Stuart Mill (*Utilitarianism*)

Mill's position seems to allow for a "yes" answer to this question, but the exercises raise the possibility that studying might, in the long run, be more "fun"—that is, more conducive to happiness—than watching television, playing computer games, and so forth.

Teaching Tips

1. Emphasize that *all eight* of the examples must be considered essential to happiness. Other types of example are possible, of course, but these eight have been chosen to represent a broad range of human activity. If students resist the specific content of an example, it should readily be possible to modify the example as stated and thereby preserve its relevance. Thus, if a student is, for example, allergic to ice cream, then replace ice cream with pizza (or whatever food is to that person's liking).

2. The activity of ranking elements of happiness is especially exciting when done in a group setting. The strategic pedagogical problem will be controlling the discussion as opinions intersect—and conflict—concerning what should be rated what as far as happiness is concerned.

3. Indicate that the ranking of the eight examples should be based on their *importance*, not necessarily on their frequency. It is important, indeed essential, to eat in order to sustain life, but it is not necessary that the food one consumes should always be to one's liking. Thus, it appears that someone could be happy while eating a very humble diet.

4. Students (of all ages) commonly say that happiness is completely subjective and that "it all depends" on what an individual likes to do. Mill's approach to happiness undercuts this relativism in two directions:

    (a) If one person harms another person because he or she thinks that the results of such harm will produce happiness (e.g., teasing or bullying), this kind of action cannot be tolerated. The pursuit of happiness, minimally, cannot entail harming others since the person harmed is thereby deprived of a measure of happiness simply by virtue of being harmed.

    (b) Mill's position claims that some types of actions are more desirable or valuable than others. If so, then we have an obligation to ourselves to spend at least some time doing things that we might not especially like doing—such as studying—but will be, in the long run, to our best interests. (See **Question #4** for discussion of duty, and of duties to oneself.)

Question #7. Should you ever tell a lie?

Immanuel Kant (*Fundamental Principles of the Metaphysics of Morals*)

The obvious answer to this question would appear to be "no." However, the exercises will be arranged in such a way as to suggest that "yes" might be an attractive alternative in some cases. The Kantian position offers an interesting and important perspective to explain and justify a "no" answer.

Teaching Tips

1. Stress the importance of answering the questions honestly. The questions lose much of their force if students answer according to some deep-seated sense of what is expected of them, rather than what, in fact, they would do.

2. Although the examples are simple, it should be noted that younger students tend to be very practical and pragmatic about details pertaining to examples. Question 5 is a case in point. Insist that the details for exactly how the wealth would be acquired are not relevant; all that counts here is that the means to attain this end—wealth—is telling a lie.

3. The key philosophical issue is whether the beneficial consequences of the act of lying override lying understood as a means to an end, given that lying is immoral. Ask the students to present reasons why consequences should take precedence over the fact that the liar is suffering some form of personal damage to his or her integrity—or nature—as a human being.

4. If the students opt for consequences as the decisive factor in determining the morality of an action, ask them to state this belief in the form of a principle (e.g., "*An action is morally good if its consequences are beneficial*"). This kind of articulation requires thinking at a fairly high level of generality but the effort to express such a principle will be invigorating and informative for both students and teacher. (For a discussion using the concepts of means and ends in a social context, see **Question #8**.)

Question #8. Are there times when you should be violent?

Martin Luther King, Jr. (Selections from speeches and writings)

Following Gandhi, King argues that violence is never justified in order to achieve social justice. Young people often experience anger (at times even violence) in arguments, and the activity will show some of the factors that must be taken into account before making a decision on this difficult question in individual, as well as in social, situations.

Teaching Tips

1. The question of whether nonviolence is the best way to achieve social justice remains in dispute. Discuss the point in class. If the class is racially and/or ethnically mixed, be ready for especially serious and passionate discussion! However, even without a racial mix this topic can arouse considerable interest and stir deep feelings among the students.

2. Students often ask whether nonviolence should be extended to cover self-defense in case of personal attack. This is a difficult question. If this problem arises, one approach is to emphasize that King's position is directed at rectifying *social* injustice and, as such, pertains to large groups of people rather than to individuals. Drawing this distinction does not answer the question about the connection between nonviolence and self-defense, but it does locate the context of discussion in an arena that remains important and eminently worth discussing.

3. Sometimes, young men get involved in fights just to prove, either to others or to themselves, that they are "men." Ask the students whether either the means or the end (or both) of such actions are morally justified.

4. Pose hypothetical examples of various types of conflicts as they might arise in the home, at school, work, and so forth, then ask the students whether they can identify and evaluate nonviolent means for resolving these conflicts.

Question #9. Do you sometimes feel weird when you are with others?
Simone de Beauvoir (*The Second Sex*)

It is no insight to observe that, when young people differing in gender, race, or nationality mix with one another, conflicts can arise. The issue here is identifying what characteristics make some people seem to be "other" than the kind of people a young person might be comfortable with and suggesting ideas for reducing this feeling of "otherness."

Teaching Tips

1. Emphasize that students should respond *only* to those situations that they have personally experienced. The examples are sufficiently broad so that most students will have experienced most of the situations.

2. **FFT 1** is aimed at *individual* differences in reacting to social situations. **FFT 2** is aimed at *group* differences in reacting to social situations. These discussions can become emotional, especially if the class is racially and/or ethnically mixed. Stress that the discussion is to identify general characteristics and tendencies based on personal experience—but not to point fingers at particular individuals. (See **Question #33** for discussion of a common logical fallacy that often arises in this kind of discussion.)

3. Harry Potter, the central protagonist in J. K. Rowling's popular *Harry Potter and the Sorcerer's Stone* (and its sequels), endures being an outsider—until, that is, he finds a home as a student in a school for wizards. Ask the students whether they can identify additional literary characters who share the burden of being "other" as an "outsider."

Question #10. Do we control technology or does technology control us?

Martin Heidegger ("The Question Concerning Technology")

Young people tend to answer this question by choosing the former alternative. But Heidegger has a way of thinking about technology where it is not self-evidently true that automobiles, jet planes, computers, video games, television, and other forms of technology are as good for us as they might seem to be.

Teaching Tips

1. Limit the number of examples of technology to 10 items, fewer if time constraints apply. Ask several students for their lists and put them on the board (the lists will overlap). Then, ask for reasons to justify saying that these items are, all things considered, either advantageous or detrimental.

2. The point of this question is to suggest the possibility that technology may not be completely under our control—that it has, in a sense, "a life of its own." The students need not agree that technology exists in such a disembodied way. As long as they can accept that technology represents something foundational about the way human beings have interacted with nature—in short, that technology is not just "a means to an end"—then this question has been philosophically successful.

Part II—Knowledge

Question #11. How do you know for certain that things move?
Zeno

Zeno's teacher, the philosopher Parmenides, tried to show that motion was an illusion. This theory may sound fantastic, but it is not, and Zeno tried to demonstrate it indirectly by constructing a series of paradoxes—Achilles and the tortoise is a famous example. The activity shows how knowing that things move involves much more than just observing objects with our eyes.

Teaching Tips

1. The standard criticism of Zeno's treatment of motion is that he has transformed a phenomenon that is *continuous* into something that is *discrete*. Just as a line is not a set of individual (or discrete) points, so also motion is not just a set of individual, and separable, units of movement. The trick is to recognize that motion is something that is inherently "on the move," as it were, and then to try to analyze this phenomenon while the motion is ongoing. Philosophically, this is not easily done.

2. **FFT 2** is intended to make students aware that knowledge is produced by mental activity, not just by the operation of the senses. We can understand the fact of motion, but this understanding must be secured through the mind in conjunction with the apparent evidence of the senses.

3. **FFT 3** will start students thinking about numbers and about mathematics generally as if it were a discipline done exclusively with the mind, rather than with visible objects. Thus, when we add numbers in arithmetic, we are not combining a group of physical objects to another group of physical objects—rather, we are performing an abstract function through the mind's understanding of certain concepts.

4. The primary point of this question is to arouse the students' interest in the problems of epistemology (i.e., in the mysterious matter of explaining how we *know* things). The teacher may, of course, pursue problematic aspects of the concept of motion as they arise from student discussion. Motion is a fascinating concept and challenging to analyze.

Question #12. What makes something you say true?
Aristotle (*Categories*)

Aristotle says that something is true if what is said, a proposition, corresponds to what is there, a fact in the world. The primary point of this question is to invite young people to recognize that truth is more than just how they feel about something they think or believe or say. Truth requires something "out there" to exist as a reality.

Teaching Tips

1. Emphasize the importance of thinking carefully before answering the questions; also, the importance of answering as honestly as possible.

2. **FFT 1** prefigures **Question #36** in the Critical Thinking section (Part IV), which concerns the logical fallacy of "*common belief.*"

3. The discussions in **FFT 1–4** are compressed. If students wish to discuss, and disagree with, the analyses presented there, by all means allow them to do so. The key point to preserve in class discussion is Aristotle's position that truth requires an objective state of affairs (i.e., a fact to which a proposition corresponds).

4. The desired philosophical point will have been made in this question if students take seriously the position that truth depends on something in the world, rather than just on personal belief—in short, that truth includes an "objective," as well as a "subjective," component.

Question #13. Can you doubt that you exist?
René Descartes (*Meditations on First Philosophy*)

This question has a bizarre feel to it, but its point is of paramount importance as far as knowledge is concerned. The activity presents opportunities to recognize the importance of the concept of *certitude*, following Descartes' highly imaginative route for arriving philosophically at the source of certitude.

Teaching Tips

1. Questions 1–3 can be readily answered "true" on condition that one is in some sort of delusional state. Students with mathematical sophistication might suggest the 3 + 2 would not equal 5 if a base other than 10 were used. Also common is the ploy that, if the symbol "3" did not mean 3 but some other number, then it is possible that 3 + 2 would not equal 5.

   Descartes' move, more subtle and ingenious, is to posit the existence of an "evil demon." Students often ask whether this is Satan, and the best answer is "no," since Descartes shows later in the *Meditations* that a being such as the evil demon could not in fact coexist with a God who is beneficent and not a deceiver. However, some of the effects the evil demon has on human beings are similar to the effects commonly attributed to Satan. In short, it may be argued that the evil demon is introduced strictly for philosophical, rather than for any covert religious purpose.

2. One way to develop **FFT 2** is to ask whether we can imagine ourselves capable of thinking if we were without a brain. If we can imagine such activity, then it is possible and, therefore, on Descartes' principles, it would follow that the mind and the brain are not identical.

3. Descartes would question the well-known distinction in current psychology between "right-brained" and "left-brained" thinking. For Descartes, if we are reasoning logically (left-brained), then the *entire mind* is thinking in this way; if we are creating a work of art (right-brained), then *all* of our mind is doing this activity. Descartes might suggest that, since we cannot be doing left-brained and right-brained activities simultaneously, one can infer that, even if one side of the brain is dominant in the origin of a certain kind of thinking, the mind as a whole—not the brain—is the conveyor of this thought.

4. To extend the mind/brain distinction into a contemporary context, see **Question #20**.

5. It is very interesting—and challenging—to investigate what happens to the subjective/objective distinction Immanuel Kant develops in **Question #16** if Descartes' position on the "thinking thing" as the origin of certainty is assumed to be correct. (Hint: What could be "objective" for Descartes?)

Question #14. Does a tree make a sound if it falls in a forest with no one around?
George ("Bishop") Berkeley (*Three Dialogues Between Hylas and Philonous*)

This bromide of a question can be answered—assuming that Berkeley's principles are correct. The answer is that we cannot tell, and his reasons are very interesting. The exercises invite students to reflect on what it means to perceive something and also what conditions must be fulfilled before perception can lead to knowledge.

Teaching Tips

1. Regarding **FFT 1**: The trick is to produce an example that is identified and described in such a way that an observer is not assumed in the identification. For as soon as the observer's presence becomes apparent, then Berkeley's position takes over! When a student suggests an intended counterexample, consider it carefully and see whether or not the student is implicitly perceiving the example in his or her description of it. If so, then the counterexample fails, and we must keep trying if we want to refute Berkeley's position.

2. Regarding **FFT 2**: The common-sense answer to (a) is surely "no." But, when (b) is discussed, the answer seems to be that we don't know for sure whether or not the earth is still there, although we certainly believe that it would not vanish! For (c), the answer Berkeley provides is that God maintains things in existence by continually perceiving—or thinking about (assuming that God does not "perceive")—everything in creation. The implication is that the earth, and of course the entire universe, will continue to exist even if human beings vanish from the scene—as long as God keeps paying attention to what God created. Thus "to be is to be perceived" still holds, only now it is God doing the perceiving, not human beings. (See **Question #26** for discussion of another issue in which God plays an essential philosophical role.)

Question #15. Are you certain that the law of gravity is really a law?
David Hume (*An Inquiry Concerning Human Understanding*)

Hume wonders whether our certainty that gravity is a law of nature is due more to habitual patterns of experience rather than to anything in nature, as such. The activity shows the close connection between the patterns of ordinary experience and what science claims is *in* the world.

Teaching Tips

1. To reinforce that statements 4–6 in the activity could actually happen, try this gambit: Hold out a piece of chalk or a marker and ask the students to imagine what *could conceivably* happen once the object is released. They quickly recognize that any number of (bizarre) things could occur: the object could rise, hover, disappear, whistle Dixie, and so forth. This approach is useful in initiating the possibility that things in the natural order could be very different from what they are. Another way to engender this approach is to recall the world as depicted in J. K. Rowling's *Harry Potter and the Sorcerer's Stone*, where a wondrous universe of wizards and magic exists side by side with the "real" world we normally inhabit. (For a more general discussion of the notion of possibility, see **Question #30**)

2. Hume's position, carried to extremes, would result in a severe form of skepticism about the results of the sciences. Ask the students whether they can identify the characteristics of science that seem to show that scientific conclusions are not merely the result of habit. Here are possible answers: the intersubjective character of experimental method, the fact that experiments are subject to repetition, the power of science to predict consequences. Any or all of these characteristics may be appealed to in this regard. In fact, Hume does not deny that gravity exists. His philosophical concern is to emphasize that when we are *certain* of something in the natural order, our certainty depends exclusively on what we have habitually experienced in nature.

Question #16. How can you tell when you know something?

Immanuel Kant (*Critique of Pure Reason*)

Toward the end of this massive work, Kant neatly summarizes his position on knowledge. The activity shows that knowledge requires an objective component (i.e., something known to be the case in the world—not just a subjective feeling of certitude on the part of the knower).

Teaching Tips

1. This approach to knowledge is similar to Aristotle's conception of truth (see **Question #12**) in that Kant emphasizes the necessity of an objective element; knowledge requires a component in addition to subjective feelings on the part of the observer. Many young people are relativists about such concepts as truth and knowledge, and the Kantian position offers them another approach to this vital set of concepts.

2. What is considered to be "objective" may be questioned by the students. The precise nature of objectivity is disputed, but the concept may be defended by appealing to kinds of evidence that are intersubjective (i.e., that do not depend just on a single observer). (See **Question #13** for a quite different approach to the concepts of objectivity and certainty.)

3. Regarding **FFT 1**: Kant explains the distinction between an opinion and a belief as follows: An *opinion* is felt to be somewhat uncertain by the individual who holds it. A *belief* is held to be certain, but there are not sufficient objective reasons to elevate that opinion into knowledge. Thus, for Kant, an opinion is weaker than a belief since an opinion lacks objective reasons to substantiate it.

4. If students challenge any aspect of the Kantian position (e.g., his use of "objective" criteria as essential to knowledge), then encourage them to try to produce their own theory of knowledge, or even an approach to the problem of knowledge that differs from Kant's. Anyone who can do this kind of thinking should be praised as an exceptionally worthy philosopher.

Question #17. Can another person understand your feelings?

Ludwig Wittgenstein (*Philosophical Investigations*)

If you feel sad and say "*I feel sad,*" how do you know that someone else can understand what you say? This problem has been analyzed in a variety of ways by contemporary philosophers following Wittgenstein's lead. The activity shows the importance of identifying our feelings as accurately as possible so that our language about these feelings will be equally accurate, or at least as accurate as language can be in these cases.

Teaching Tips

1. If students select an answer other than sadness, let them proceed with whatever alternative is chosen. Making this substitution in the activity is straightforward and easily done.

2. Stress that there are no right or wrong answers for the activity. The purpose is to have students reflect on the relation between language and their feelings and to try to evoke those feelings through words as accurately and vividly as possible.

3. Class discussion of the results of the activity is fascinating. Advise the students to be thoughtful and charitable in their remarks on the contributions of their peers. If the class reaches a favorable consensus on a given word or phrase, the implication is that the author has seen an important connection between the language game involving the word for a certain feeling (e.g., "sadness") and the feeling itself. (There might also be a budding poet in your midst!)

4. **FFT 4** is useful for contrasting how language evokes feelings compared to other media. As a footnote, the question of whether works of art "express" emotions has been the subject of much discussion in *aesthetics*, the area in philosophy that studies the concepts of art and beauty. Asking the students whether a poem or a piece of music more adequately conveys an emotion will engender considerable interest—and argument!

Question #18. Can you lie to yourself?
Jean-Paul Sartre (*Being and Nothingness*)

One of Sartre's most intriguing theories is that we do, in fact, lie to ourselves and that we do so frequently. The activity illustrates to young people that being truly honest with oneself about one's feelings and attitudes is often difficult—and also very important.

Teaching Tips

1. Emphasize that Sartre's version of existentialism is only one of many different philosophies that fall under this rubric. *Being and Nothingness* is a long work, and it includes a considerable amount of technical language (as does a great deal of contemporary philosophy). However, the examples Sartre provides to illustrate his concepts are usually vivid and impressive. Sartre won the Nobel Prize for Literature in 1965—and declined the award as a gesture incompatible with his Marxist principles.

2. Three reactions are given in Example B. Ask the students whether other feasible reactions are possible and, if so, whether they should be included as options in this activity.

3. According to published reports, children are starting to smoke at increasingly younger ages. If it happens that students are already smoking, ask them to recall as best they can what their first experiences with smoking were like and then use this experience in their response to Example B.

4. If we feel a certain way about something or somebody, is it possible for us to tell ourselves that we *don't* feel that way and to believe that what we are telling ourselves is so? This intriguing question may be considered in conjunction with **Question #17** and its concern for the possibility that another person can understand what we are feeling.

Question #19. Do you perceive things as they really are or only as they seem to be?
Bertrand Russell (*The Problems of Philosophy*)

Russell opens his discussion of the major problems of philosophy by stating the theory of "sense-data." This position says that we perceive data that our senses relay to our minds. The activity raises the question of whether or not what we are perceiving really does exist independently of our sensory and perceptual experience.

Teaching Tips

1. Emphasize the importance of describing only what is *seen*. For example, the word "desk" should not be used in the description since the student as observer *knows* that it is a desk, but that is not what he or she *sees*. The mind supplies the word "desk" to refer to a perceived object of a certain shape and size.

2. Sight is the sense used here in the discussion, but the theory of sense-data encompasses all the senses. Thus, what is heard, felt, and so forth, will vary from person to person, just as what is seen.

3. **FFT 1** raises issues that, as noted, establish links to **Questions #23** and **#24**. Consider examining either (or both) of these questions if the students are intrigued by the appearance/reality distinction.

4. **FFT 2** suggests that microscopic data are no more reliable than data gathered by the naked eye. This implication is fascinating since we tend to believe that only scientific investigation reveals what things "really" are.

Question #20. Can computers think?
Daniel Dennett (*Consciousness Explained*)

There are many discussions of this important question by contemporary philosophers, with Dennett one of the most prominent. The exercises allow the student to recognize some of the conditions that must be present before "thinking" can be said to occur—an inquiry that must be pursued before the question about computers and thought can be properly answered.

Teaching Tips

1. **FFT 1** asks students to do better at composing the activity than the author—a challenge they will certainly enjoy! However, it is the teacher's responsibility to evaluate their suggestions by determining whether they are significantly different from the types of activity given in the five propositions.

2. It is possible that science will never fully comprehend the workings of the brain. But, to hold this opinion based solely on the incomplete status of present research and knowledge is to cling to the notion, essentially romantic in cast, that something uniquely individual defines our nature as human beings. If students maintain that science will never fully understand the brain, the burden is on them to indicate what kind of activity we perform as human beings that is, in principle, closed off to any and all future brain research. This is an interesting and subtle issue, and it forms a link to **Question #17**, which concerns the relationship between language and human feeling.

Part III—Reality

Question #21. Can you think about nothing at all?
Parmenides

The early Greek thinkers had difficulty understanding the meaning of "not," as in "*He is not a good student.*" Parmenides offers interesting reasons to explain the ultimate meanings of "not" and "nothing," and the activity demonstrates this intriguing function.

Teaching Tips

1. Regarding **FFT 1**: Although centaurs do not exist in the world (as far as we know), they do exist mythically. So, if one's metaphysics allows the existence of mythical beings, then meaningful propositions about centaurs are possible. (See **Question #24** for discussion of different senses of existence, an important issue in metaphysics.)

2. See **Question #38** on the Liar Paradox for another pivotal application of the meaning/reference distinction.

3. If students are stumped by the meaning of "not," there should be no cause for concern. The first legitimate interpretation of "not" did not occur until Plato, late in life, wrote the dialogue called *Sophist*. In this work, Socrates explains that one primary meaning of "not," as in the sentence "Athens is not New York," is "other than." Thus when we deny that something is the case, we are saying that X is "other than" Y. For example, "Athens is not New York" is equivalent to "Athens is other than New York." However, the function of the concept of negation—as in the words "nothing," "not," and so forth—is complex, and the Platonic response in the *Sophist*, although original and profound, tells only part of the story.

4. If students have read *Harry Potter and the Sorcerer's Stone*, they will probably recall the following incident (and, even if they have not, the exchange is self-contained and provides a ready opportunity for an enjoyable and provocative exploration of the relevant philosophical point). Reproduce this conversation and see whether the students can figure out why the exchange is humorous (and frustrating to Filch!).

When Harry and some friends are being chased by the villainous Filch, the following interchange occurs between Filch and Peeves, the gatekeeper, just as Filch is closing in fast on our young hero:

"Which way did they go, Peeves?" Filch was saying. "Quick, tell me."
"Say 'please.'"
"Don't mess with me, Peeves, now *where did they go?*"
"Shan't say nothing if you don't say please," said Peeves in his annoying singsong voice.
"All right—*please.*"
"Nothing! Ha haaa! Told you I wouldn't say nothing if you didn't say please! Ha ha! Haaaaaa!" And they [Harry and friends] heard the sound of Peeves whooshing away and Filch cursing in rage.

Here is a philosophical way to untangle this exchange: When Peeves says he "shan't say nothing if you don't say please," Filch takes him to mean that Peeves will not speak anything unless Filch prefaces his request with a polite "please." But, when Filch dutifully says "please," Peeves responds with "Nothing" (i.e., the *word* "nothing," not the meaningful information concerning Harry's whereabouts that Filch had anticipated). Peeves has deviously collapsed the distinction between meaning and reference—as things turn out, his response to Filch *referred to* the *word* nothing itself whereas Filch took Peeves' usage of nothing to *mean* the absence of speech altogether. This delicious episode, neatly and subtly interlaced with logical and metaphysical bite, is only one small sample of the many philosophical dimensions that permeate this wonderful piece of fiction.

Question #22. Does anything ever happen by chance?
Democritus

The first systematic attempt in western philosophy at materialism developed in terms of atoms. This position suggests that everything happens necessarily by virtue of the activity of atoms. The activity focuses attention on the concept of chance and whether, according to Democritus' principles, this concept is meaningful.

Teaching Tips

1. If everything is determined, then the notion of free will seems difficult to maintain. This implication is a good example of the intimacy between metaphysics and ethics. Democritus' theory of atoms (metaphysics) appears to render it difficult to maintain that a "free choice" makes any sense (ethics). See **Question #28** for a discussion of the concept of free will approached from a different perspective.

2. Regarding **FFT 2**: If matter included an essential dimension of randomness or disorder, then it seems that chance events could occur. This is one interpretation of reality that would justify the conclusion that chance events are possible.

3. Regarding **FFT 3**: The burden of proof seems to be on Democritus since it is difficult to see why classes of things should exist unless there was some sort of regularity in the motions of the atoms. The question of the existence of classes is always difficult for metaphysicians to resolve.

4. **FFT 4** is open-ended as far as answers are concerned. This question is useful for eliciting the students' attitudes about science and whether science has any "ultimate" goal as far as its explanations are concerned. Care should be taken to evaluate critically students' responses, regardless of whether they are affirmative or negative.

5. A fascinating and challenging question is to ask the students whether they can provide an explanation about the ultimate *origin* of Democritus' mechanical causes. What has made the atoms do what they do? Expect a variety of answers to this question and then keep the point of the question in mind as a relevant prelude to **Question #26**.

Question #23. What happens to numbers when you are not using them?
Plato (*Phaedo*)

For Plato, numbers exist apart from minds thinking about them. Most kids believe that numbers exist in the mind and nowhere else. The activity suggests that this belief should be examined with care.

Teaching Tips

1. Regarding **FFT 1**: One approach is through *conventionalism*, the theory that contends that numbers and mathematical concepts generally are the product of, and are defined by, convention. In other words, mathematicians agree among themselves that certain basic concepts will have a certain meaning. This theory is obviously far removed from the Platonic position.

2. Plato did not think of the natural numbers as a sequence defined essentially in terms of each number's successor. Regardless of how this question is resolved, whether mathematical entities exist by themselves or whether they require a mind thinking about them still remains a problem in metaphysics.

3. In general, is it necessary that a mind be thinking about something in order to guarantee that this something exists? For discussion of a theory maintaining that the mind is required to justify the existence of anything, see **Question #14**.

Question #24. Are numbers and people equally real?
Aristotle (*Metaphysics*)

Compare the number 5 and a basketball team—are they real in the same way? One of Aristotle's most fundamental principles is that *"being can be said in many ways,"* and the activity invites young people to appreciate how reality is characterized by a variety of different shades, some of them subtle and not easily recognized.

Teaching Tips

1. This chapter revolves around one of the most abstract questions in *Philosophy for Kids*. Nevertheless, it strikes a responsive chord in young people. Discussion should aim at clarifying the different senses of reality that are operating in the minds of the students, rather than at securing anything like tenable answers to the metaphysical issues sketched here.

2. Regarding **FFT 1**: If numbers are considered to be eternal, then it is possible to argue that anything marked by eternity—like a number—is "more real" than a being that is limited by a finite existence. The strength of this position rests on the belief that continuing existence is in some sense "better" than discontinued existence. (But, be prepared for an argument if you decide to defend this position!)

3. Regarding **FFT 2**: If human beings are more complex than stones (i.e., possess more distinct types of properties), then one could claim that humans are "more real" than stones. This position rests on the belief that complexity confers a different—and higher—degree of reality on a being that possesses it compared to a being that does not possess it.

4. If students find this question of interest, ask whether anyone can define reality. Write the first six or so answers on the board and then have the class critically evaluate these definitions.

Question #25. Is time what you see when you look at a clock?
St. Augustine (*Confessions*)

Time provides the "stuff" of our ordinary experience, but we rarely think about what it is. Augustine argues that time exists only in the mind, and the exercises give young people the opportunity to test that position.

Teaching Tips

1. This topic is a big favorite among students. They are convinced that Augustine's position is incorrect, but they find it difficult to show why they believe this is so. For example, one popular gambit is to appeal to the fossil record concerning dinosaurs. If dinosaurs have become extinct, doesn't that prove that time exists outside of our minds? The answer: It does not! The fossil record must be interpreted, and, when it is, human minds do the interpreting. As soon as human beings say that dinosaurs existed "millions of years ago," this vast reach of time exists—in the minds of humans! Augustine would not deny that dinosaurs existed and are now extinct. He would deny that time existed while the dinosaurs roamed the earth since there were no human observers during that period of earthly activity. Motion (e.g., of the dinosaurs) and time are distinct from one another as concepts in metaphysics—as well as in reality!

2. Regarding **FFT 2**: This is a key question and one that, if developed, suggests that Augustine's account of time is incomplete. But, if time is not thought of, with Augustine, as a purely human concept, then it appears as if it must be some sort of fundamental "given," as a component in a primordial space-time continuum. Those students with a special interest in science will find this question fascinating to pursue.

3. For an accessible and informative discussion of current approaches to the concept of time (including a neatly relevant quote from St. Augustine), see "The Riddle of Time" by Michael D. Lemonick in *Time*, December 27, 1999, pp. 142–144.

Question #26. If the universe came from the Big Bang, where did the Big Bang come from?
St. Thomas Aquinas (*Summa Theologica*)

Aquinas indirectly anticipates and criticizes the "Big Bang" theory by arguing that any order that exists in the universe must have had a designer (i.e., God). The activities show how the Big Bang theory is apparently incomplete since Aquinas would argue that the stuff of the Big Bang must be created by a supremely intelligent being—God.

Teaching Tips

1. The device of introducing a parallel universe raises the question about the nature of time in a universe in which human beings have not yet appeared. Thus, according to St. Augustine, time would not exist in such a universe (**Question #25**)! **Questions #25** and **#26** form a close thematic pair and are fascinating to do in sequence.

2. Care should be exercised when discussing God since, for many students, this is an emotional issue. Emphasize that the discussion is strictly philosophical and that it is definitely not intended to affect anyone's religious beliefs. (As an aside, it is a constant source of wonder to the author how many sixth, seventh, and eighth graders are avowed atheists, or at least claim they are. Be prepared to deal with individuals who will vigorously deny the existence of God!)

3. The question in **FFT 1** is effectively answered in **FFT 2**. But, see how the students do with this question on their own, prior to examining **FFT 2**.

4. The question "*But who created God?*" is often asked by students. The answer (according to Aquinas): no one. God always was, is, and will be; in a word, it is part of God's nature to be eternal. Strictly speaking, this question is off the point since Aquinas' Five Ways are intended to demonstrate only that God exists; they are not intended to display a full account of the nature of God. However, in the course of discussion of Aquinas' argument, students often display a keen desire to talk about the nature of God. The teacher must be firm in distinguishing between God's existence and God's nature. A footnote: Aquinas spends considerable time in the *Summa Theologica* describing the nature of God, so students are perfectly justified in their concern about

165

this issue. But, it is axiomatic in philosophy that one cannot say everything at once, and this is a good case in point. Questions pertaining to God's *existence* are separate from questions pertaining to God's *nature*.

5. Regarding **FFT 3**: If matter is eternal, then the argument from design is seriously damaged. Cosmologists argue that, over vast reaches of time, it is possible that eternal matter can randomly form something as complex as the universe. If so, then a deity is not required to provide the original cosmic blueprint, as it were. This question continues to spark long and heated debate among experts. Do not expect to resolve it, just to clarify what the students are thinking about this issue. (This topic is always a big favorite among students.)

Question #27. Are you the same person you were five years ago?
John Locke (*Essay Concerning Human Understanding*)

Well, yes and no. The philosophical trick is to be clear on what is the same and what is not the same about a person. Locke's answer concerns a certain theoretical understanding of consciousness and self-awareness; the activities help foster this sense of awareness.

Teaching Tips

1. Regarding **FFT 1**: Locke might respond that it is the *content* of our memories, not their qualitative *strength or weakness* in our mind, that guarantees our identity as a unique person. A hazy memory remains a memory—the uniqueness of this memory is what Locke emphasizes in the present context.

2. What makes a young person a unique individual is a topic of natural and enduring interest, especially at this age, since the very nature of the issue allows students to think at length about themselves. Thus, if students wish to contest Locke's position on personal identity, allow them to have their say. It is a good exercise in critical thinking to have the class evaluate any alternative theory using Locke's position on memory as the standard of explanation.

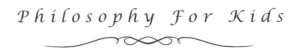

Question #28. Do you have a free will?
Thomas Hobbes

This is a venerable question in ethics that remains important in a number of fundamental moral contexts (e.g., whether human beings should be held responsible for their actions). A common sense answer is yes, we do have free will. However, the activity leads students to a point at which they will be receptive to Hobbes' denial of free will.

Teaching Tips

1. Regarding **FFT 2**: Hobbes contends that punishment, even if in some sense unjustified from the standpoint of the lack of free will, remains meritorious in society insofar as it serves as a deterrent. In other words, people who may be tempted to act unjustly might decide not to do so if they think of the unpleasantness of society's punishments assuming they were to act in this way—and get caught!

2. The quotation from Samuel Johnson at the head of this chapter is well-known. Ask the students whether the good doctor's quip—a brusque dismissal of the question by the simple assertion, without benefit of argument, that free will exists—has any philosophical merit. Thus, if I feel that I have free will, is that feeling sufficient evidence to justify the belief that I do, in fact, have free will?

Question #29. Does anything depend on everything?
Georg Hegel (*The Science of Logic*)

Any well-adjusted individual realizes that he or she depends on many other people and things in order to survive, much less to be happy. But, are there limits to such dependency? In Hegel's view of the world, everything is linked to every other thing at a fundamental level that the philosopher must discover and describe. The activity helps students appreciate this position, beautiful in its abstractness.

Teaching Tips

1. Regarding **FFT 1**: Hegel's position does not require that we know everything there is to know about everything (or even that we know everything there is to know about any one thing). It does require that the reality of any given thing be defined so that this thing's individuality is necessarily connected to every other dimension of reality. So, the fact that any one human being cannot know everything there is to know does not, by itself, refute Hegel's metaphysical concern for, and emphasis on, totality.

2. Regarding **FFT 2**: From Hegel's standpoint, any true proposition that referred to a particular being would be only a *partial* truth since this proposition would not make explicit the relations between that being and all other beings. This approach is usually called the *coherence theory of truth*, implying that truth in the most precise sense must demonstrate how each particular thing "coheres with" all other things. Most contemporary philosophers believe that the *correspondence theory of truth* (see **Question #12**) is closer to the usual sense of the term "truth" than its principal rival, the coherence theory of truth. Also, the coherence theory of truth is generally considered to be more difficult to defend against objections than the correspondence theory of truth.

Question #30. Are impossible things ever possible?

If round squares are impossible, are they impossible for the same reason that motion faster than the speed of light is impossible? The activity helps demonstrate that the concepts of possibility and impossibility have a number of different meanings.

Teaching Tips

1. Regarding **FFT 1**: The discussion in this chapter offers material that is sufficient to provide an evaluation of this bromide.

2. Regarding **FFT 2**: A contradiction is so devastating because it is, in a real sense, self-nullifying. Consider "*This ball is red and this ball is not red.*" Since no such ball could exist, this proposition does not—and cannot—refer to anything. So, if a philosopher were guilty of a contradiction, then it would be as if the philosopher had never said anything at all! Philosophers, like most people, would like their views to be heard and discussed by others. But, if a philosopher generated a contradiction, then no one would want to listen to that philosopher for the simple reason that the philosopher had never really said anything in the first place!

   Trying to show that a philosopher's writings contain a contradiction (or, even worse, multiple contradictions) is one of the most common forms of philosophical criticism. The articles that appear in philosophical journals—and at this point of the new millennium, there are over 200 such journals—are rife with this strategy.

Part IV—Critical Thinking

Question #31. Is it important to speak and write so you can be understood?

Playing with words is fun; but, as a rule, words are serious. The activity emphasizes the importance of being as clear as possible when we think, speak, and write.

Teaching Tips

1. This activity works well in the classroom. Have a student read proposition 1, making sure that the student emphasizes the word in italics. Then, ask the class for the meaning of the proposition when it is read with this kind of emphasis. As the five versions of the proposition are read and the various meanings indicated, jot down the different meanings on the board.

2. For an extension of the point made in this exercise, ask the students to give an example of a proposition that is ambiguous because of misplaced wording. This is called the fallacy of *amphiboly* (i.e., where a proposition becomes confusing because of "two in a lump"—the literal meaning of the Greek word from which the term *amphiboly* is derived). This fallacy occurs when poorly placed words or phrases make a proposition "lumpy" and, therefore, uneven, obscure, or even comical in meaning. (*The New Yorker* is fond of using amphibolies as fillers at the end of articles.)

Question #32. Should you always listen to the opinions of others?

It seems obvious that the answer is "yes," but young people are often impatient when it comes to paying attention to someone else, especially if the other person has an opposed view. The exercise elicits an understanding and appreciation of this subtle point.

Teaching Tips

1. Although the topics of the 10 opinions range widely and generally pertain to young people, some students may have no interest whatsoever in a given opinion (or opinions) among those presented in the activity. These individuals will tend to answer "no" for those opinions. Therefore, if a student gives, for example, six "yes" answers, it does not necessarily follow that this student has a relatively narrow range of interests and would not listen to the opinions of others. Students must be encouraged not to miss the point of the activity—that they should be willing to listen to others, even, and perhaps especially, when they are not directly or immediately interested in the topic being discussed.

2. Students may want to debate some (or all) of the opinions given in the activity. This is good in that it exemplifies the ultimate purpose of **Question #32**, but the primary point of the activity is, again, only to impress on students that it is in their long-range best interests to listen to what other people have to say. Use your discretion as far as allowing debate on a given opinion to proceed.

Question #33. Should you criticize people or the opinions people have?

In any serious discussion, it is important to distinguish between people and their ideas or beliefs. The activity shows how to appreciate this distinction as a practical prerequisite for rational discussion of issues, rather than attacks against the people who are maintaining positions on these issues.

Teaching Tips

1. Emphasize to the students the need to think about what is being discussed in each of the three sets of responses. Have them look carefully at the statements by Mary, Adolf, and Jenny, then look just as carefully at how Bill, Josef, and Jill respond to these statements.

2. The brief discussions of the three responses are intended to illustrate the point of the fallacy—that the respondent has been guilty of what logic textbooks call an *ad hominem* argument. That is, the respondent has directed a critical comment "to the person," not to the point being discussed. Feel free to expand on these discussions if necessary to make the distinction between (a) attacking a person and (b) critically evaluating that person's position.

3. Regarding **FFT 3**: *Ad hominem* responses are common in politics and also in certain legal proceedings when an attorney discredits the testimony of a witness. To discuss these usages of "attacking the person" is an interesting and rewarding extension of the point of the activity.

Question #34. Why is "because" such an important word?

A firm grasp of the word "because" is essential for critical thinking. The activity illustrates a number of the different senses of the word "because" in explaining or justifying a belief about an aspect of human nature that is usually of interest to students.

Teaching Tips

1. "Reason" as a synonym for "explanation" should be distinguished from *reasoning*, which is the movement of the mind from premises to a conclusion. Thus, to give a reason for something would not necessarily involve reasoning. However, although the activity in this chapter emphasizes giving reasons for a specific proposition, *reasoning* (in the broader, logical sense) will always be necessary in order to justify a given *reason* (in the narrower, explanatory sense).

2. Select the reason that seems to excite the most interest and discuss it in class. Also, see whether students think that other reasons should be added in order to explain intelligence adequately. A fascinating discussion can be produced by trying to explain intelligence using whatever reasons can be provided either from the activity or reasons introduced by the students. This discussion will doubtless not reach consensus—indeed, consensus in philosophy is rare—but, the students will find it an invaluable exercise in order to appreciate this complex concept. (See **Question #3** for another issue in which the concept of intelligence is crucial.)

3. For an extended discussion along the same lines as the title question, ask the students "*Why is 'why' such an important word?*" A sentence beginning with "why" is often a sentence expressing wonder about something. These are precisely the kind of sentences that can rouse interest in the adventure of philosophy. "Why" is a very important word indeed!

Question #35. Is it always easy to tell what causes things to happen?

Explaining events in terms of cause and effect appears to be a natural function of human intelligence. However, we frequently fix on a given cause too quickly, without adequate thought. This is the fallacy of "questionable cause." The activity presents a series of examples illustrating this tendency and the discussion alerts students to the need to proceed with care when stating a causal relationship.

Teaching Tips

1. The activity involves reviewing the 12 explanations and then determining the underlying pattern. Students will readily identify the pattern. The point of the activity is then to be in a position to evaluate the explanations in terms of whether or not the causal links stated in the explanations are indeed justified.

2. If students do the ranking of types of activity in **FFT 1**, be prepared for divergent responses. Students typically differ widely as to which areas they believe offer more or less certitude as far as causal certainty is concerned. If you tabulate the results of the ranking, consider discussing why students ranked the activities as they did. This discussion will bring out the students' understanding of the general difference between knowledge and opinion with respect to using the principle of cause and effect.

Question #36. If many people believe something is true, is it true?

This discussion demonstrates the logical fallacy known as "common belief" (i.e., just because many people think something is true, it does not follow that it is true just for that reason).

Teaching Tips

1. Emphasize that students are not asked whether they believe the opinions listed in the activity, but whether they think that some, many, or all people would believe these opinions. Thus, students look at each opinion and then gauge their response based on how they see people in general reacting to that opinion.

2. **FFT 1** is intended to illustrate the distinction between the *content* of an opinion and people's *reaction* to this content. For example, Michael Jordan was extremely visible as an athlete, and people can react to their actually experienced impressions of what he did. By contrast, however, God is invisible (at least as God is typically conceived); thus, the opinion "God exists" operates on a different level of experience.

3. The point of **FFT 2** is based, as was **FFT 1**, on the distinction between the content of an opinion and people's reaction to that content. If the opinion concerns an attitude or human activity, then it is possible that the way people perceive or respond to this opinion will have a bearing concerning the opinion's truth. Thus, will it be the case that "practice *always* make perfect?" It seems as if natural ability will necessarily set limits on how much perfection human endeavor can achieve.

Question #37. Do two wrongs balance out and make an action right?

The activity and discussion illustrate the logical fallacy known as "*two wrongs make a right,*" a strategy of justification quite common among young people. ("*Well, he did it too!*")

Teaching Tips

1. Stress that the underlying pattern of the five examples will become apparent only after the sequence has been examined as a complete set. If the students do not detect the pattern, it is explained in **FFT 4**. Note that it is not essential to the overall point of **Question #37** that this pattern be made explicit.

2. Emphasize that "acceptable" in the five examples means *morally* acceptable. The point here is not what *would* you do in this situation; rather, what *should* you do.

3. **FFT 1–3** are intended to justify the conclusions stated. However, if students want to question and then debate the reasoning in any of these discussions, encourage them to do so.

4. If the students argue that the circumstances described in Example 5 imply that "*two wrongs don't make a right*" does not hold in this case, request that they state their reasons. This discussion may (and probably will) reinforce the approach to morality based on consequences. Thus if the principle of "*two wrongs don't make a right*" were applied slavishly and our country was destroyed as a result, it is not clear that our decision was, in fact, morally correct. (See **Question #6** for an approach to morality that is relevant in this case.)

   Note that the discussion in **FFT 4** concludes on an indeterminate note. The students should be convinced that "*two wrongs . . .*" is an acceptable moral principle in *many* cases, but that it might not be a hard-and-fast rule to be applied in *all* cases.

5. A fruitful illustration and application of the logical force of this fallacy emerges from **Question #8** and its concern for redressing violence through nonviolent means. If a group of people has been treated unjustly and harmed with violence, do these people have the right to react in the same way toward the individuals who have so treated them? Do two wrongs make a right?

Question #38. "I am lying." True or false?

This is a famous logical paradox, over 2,000 years old, familiarly known as the "Liar Paradox." Many similar versions of it exist and are still used today as puzzles. (As an aside, it drives kids crazy—its resolution also exercised philosophers until well into the 20th century.) The activity introduces the basic distinctions between true and false propositions and also between meaning and reference in a proposition.

Teaching Tips

1. The paragraph after "*I am lying*" is compressed in summarizing the paradox, but it usually suffices to show the logical alternatives.

2. The word *paradox* has a number of meanings, most of them without logical rigor. But the paradoxical character of the Liar Paradox is clear and precise, which is why logicians and philosophers have found it so fertile and worthy of serious study. For a very different kind of paradox, equally important in the area of metaphysics, see **Question #11**.

3. Ideally, the students performing the skit should have some facility in staccato delivery, since the Samuel Beckett-like quality of the responses is increased if they emerge rapid-fire. The classic Abbot and Costello "*Who's on first?*" can be used as a model. By the way, this routine trades almost exclusively on the property of self-reference for its humor (although it is probably true that this famed comic duo was more interested in entertaining than in making any subtle philosophical points).

4. Regarding **FFT 4**: Reasoning can occur with only *one* premiss, although most of the reasoning we do, practical and theoretical, contains two (or more) premisses.

5. If students firmly grasp the difference between the meaning of what they say or write and what their discourse *refers to*, then the activity, and the Liar Paradox, have served their purpose. Thus, the question "*What do you mean?*" cannot be answered by pointing to what the challenged statement refers. The meaning of the statement must be analyzed and then clarified.

Question #39. Can something logical ever not make sense?

This discussion introduces the basic logical concept of *validity*—formal conditions that make an argument logically correct even if the content of the argument is bizarre, if not loony. The examples here are entertaining in establishing this relatively abstract concept in logic.

Teaching Tips

1. Reasoning, understood in a logical context, is normally defined as connecting propositions (i.e., sentences) as premises in order to produce a conclusion that provides new information.

2. Emphasize that this activity will focus on the *form* of the sentences rather than on their content. The concept of validity in logic depends on abstracting from the content of propositions and recognizing how they, the propositions, are formally constructed. As the activity proceeds, the concept of *form* is often-mentioned and illustrated.

3. Do not be concerned if students do not immediately grasp the relevance of "If it is true that . . ." The point will be explained later in the discussion.

4. Regarding **FFT 1**: Reasoning can be valid without being *sound*—Example 2 is a case in point. A sound argument is a valid argument with true premises (e.g., Example 1). Thus, all sound arguments are valid, but not all valid arguments are sound.

5. Regarding **FFT 2**: As a rule, we want reasoning to produce propositions that are true. Thus, we do not want just to reason validly; rather, we want our reasoning to be sound, as well.

6. Regarding **FFT 3**: Possibilities of invalid reasoning are endless due to improper arrangement and connection of classes. Here is one:

All cats are animals.
All dogs are animals.
Therefore, all cats are dogs.

Ask the students whether they can diagnose what has gone wrong in this argument. (Answer: The class of all cats and the class of all dogs do not jointly exhaust the class of animals. Therefore, it is *formally* incorrect—because of incorrect assumptions about the classes in this argument—to identify cats with dogs as claimed by the argument's conclusion. Furthermore, *any* argument of this form would be equally invalid, regardless of the content of the propositions.)

Question #40. "I wonder . . . what it means to define something?"

This, the concluding activity, focuses on the question of what it means to define a term. Four types of definitions are described, with the exercises intended to give students practice in recognizing examples of these types.

Teaching Tips

1. Other examples showing any or all of the four types of definitions may be substituted if replacement seems warranted for greater relevance. The point of this question is to provide theoretical background for recognizing differences among types of definitions and to practice identifying instances of these types. The particular examples are not as important as the *differences* between and among the examples as instances of definitions.

2. The answers are:
   stipulative = black hole;
   lexical = centaur;
   theoretical = heat; and
   persuasive = capitalism.

3. Take two standard dictionaries and check their definitions of terms important in philosophy (e.g., justice, time, friendship, and so forth). Ask the students to compare the two definitions and use their critical thinking skills to evaluate them philosophically. This exercise is challenging and great fun for students since they will be critiquing the same reference works that they often use to settle arguments about meanings of terms!

Curricular Integration

The following suggestions are for integrating the 40 questions into the curriculum. Creative teachers will discover many more than those listed below!

Language Arts

The section on *Critical Thinking*, **Questions #31–40**, can be used either in its entirety, in selected groups or singly as preparation for expository writing or for debate-type discussions. The exception is, perhaps, **Question #38**, a famous (and over 2,000-year-old) logical paradox that causes much consternation—and exuberant fun—when students try to unravel it. But, for adventurous teachers, include **Question #38** as well! Also useful:

- **Questions #12** and **#16** as preludes to expository writing based on facts.

- **Question #17** for fictional or poetic writing exercises.

Mathematics

- **Questions #23** and **#24** inspire a thoughtful attitude toward basic concepts in arithmetic or algebra.

- **Question #25** helps show the connection between numerical measurement and time.

Science

- **Question #25** when studying types of motion in natural processes.

- **Question #26** for discussions about the origin of the universe or topics pertaining to evolution.

- **Question #15** to initiate a discussion of the place of law in science.

- **Questions #22** and **#35** for discussing whether it is possible for science to explain everything.

Social Studies

- **Questions #8** and **#9** as introductions to the importance of social justice and the question of the best way to attain it.

- **Question #5** is pertinent to the concept of civic responsibility or discussions of social welfare.

Special Occasions

- **Questions #3**, **#4**, and **#6** at the start of the school year as ways to instill a proper attitude for the year's work.

- **Questions #1** and **#2** for conflict resolution situations.

- **Question #10** if technological equipment is added to the classroom and **Question #20** if this equipment is a computer.

- **Questions #8** and **#9** are appropriate for Martin Luther King, Jr.'s holiday.

- **Question #27** on a student's birthday—although discretion is advised here!

Additional Reading
in Philosophy

The following works are recommended to give young people additional experience with philosophy:

Sophie's World: A Novel about the History of Philosophy
by Jostein Gaarder
New York: Berkley Books, 1996

A world-wide best-selling work, this book is a remarkable blend of philosophy and an imaginative story involving a young girl and her adventures with a gentle, but somewhat mysterious, philosophy teacher. The accounts of philosophers begin with the Greeks, cover the entire history of philosophy and are noteworthy for their accuracy and fairness. Also interspersed into the development of the plot are more general discussions of cultural, social, and religious factors relevant to the progression of philosophy. Highly recommended as a source for young people who would like to know more about philosophy.

The Story of Philosophy: The Lives and Opinions of the Great Philosophers
by Will Durant
S & S Trade, 1967

This is an extremely readable and accurate account of the history of philosophy, with additional biographical features relevant to the philosophers themselves. A good source to provide a more challenging and concentrated review of philosophy than the more generalized accounts given in *Sophie's World*.

The Problems of Philosophy
by Bertrand Russell
London: Oxford University Press, 1959

This famous little book, by one of the great mathematician-philosophers of the 20th century, is a lucid description of the major problems that have occupied philosophers since the Greeks (e.g., appearance and reality, truth and falsehood, knowledge and opinion). There is also a splendid concluding chapter on the value of philosophy. Russell was mordantly witty when he wanted to be, but here he restricts himself to laying out philosophical problems in clear and carefully modulated prose. Recommended for slightly older (or more advanced younger) students.

Irrational Man: A Study in Existential Philosophy
by William Barrett
New York: Doubleday, 1962

Existentialism is one of the most important movements in 20th-century philosophy, and Barrett's work is generally acknowledged as one of the clearest and most accessible treatments of the major figures in existentialism: Kierkegaard, Nietzsche, Sartre, Heidegger. The work also includes considerable analysis of the background conditions from which existentialism arose. Barrett's prose is clear, and he is sympathetic to the way the existentialists approached and analyzed the problems that drew them to philosophy. Younger students who had read, or even merely read in, Russell and Barrett would have secured a solid background in philosophical issues and in the existentialist perspective on these issues.

What is the Name of this Book? The Riddle of Dracula and other Logical Puzzles
by Raymond Smullyan
New York: Simon & Schuster, 1986

This is a "fun" book that subtly introduces a host of philosophical problems through several hundred logical puzzles and paradoxes. Smullyan writes clearly, with an irrepressible sense of humor. Students who like logic and critical thinking would enjoy this book—and they would also learn a great deal about logic and language. The complexity of some puzzles and paradoxes may be more appropriate for older students but the bulk of the book could be read, and savored, by younger students (and by curious adults!).

There are Two Errors in the the Title of this Book:
A Source Book of Philosophical Puzzles, Paradoxes, and Problems
by Robert M. Martin
Peterborough: Broadview Press, 1992

Martin's book is organized around a series of basic philosophical issues and concepts, although the discussions of the puzzles and paradoxes are typically longer and more detailed than in Smullyan. Martin frequently identifies the philosophers whose positions he is sketching, a useful practice for anyone wanting to pursue the philosophical theories underlying the puzzles and paradoxes.

Martin also writes clearly and in a style frequently punctuated with a sense of irony. However, his prose tends to be somewhat more difficult because he has attempted to introduce more substantial philosophy into the content of his book. Students who find Smullyan interesting and provocative can be expected to enjoy the challenge of Martin's work. (N.B.: The "the the" in the title is *not* a typo!)

Open Minds and Everyday Reasoning
by Zachary Seech
Belmont, CA: Wadsworth Publishing Co., 1993

This is an introductory logic text intended for a wide audience (the work was field tested in a California middle school). The writing is straightforward and accurate. Seech explains basic logical concepts—argument, premiss, conclusion, validity—in a way that should inform younger students willing to work independently. The chapter on informal fallacies is especially well-done and would be very useful as a complement to the Critical Thinking section in *Philosophy for Kids*. Recommended for older students, especially those with experience with, or affinity for, self-taught education.

The Little Prince
by Antoine de Saint-Exupéry (Trans. by Katherine Woods)
New York: HarBrace, 1968.

This timeless work beguiles and educates the reader on a number of levels, one of which is decidedly philosophical. The prince, the fox, the snake, the rose, and the aviator all interact to present a number of thoughtful positions on friendship, love, and dealing with "the other." Highly recommended for students who like to think deeply about important issues that originate from a literary—and, in this case, fanciful—narrative.

The Stranger
by Albert Camus
New York: Random House, 1946.

A 20th-century classic animating a completely different world from *The Little Prince* and *Harry Potter*. Meursault, the hero (or, perhaps, anti-hero), drifts through his world with no apparent deep feelings for anything. However, he is trapped in a complex set of life-and-death circumstances during which he discovers a number of important facts—many philosophical in scope.

Recommended for older students (and mature younger ones) as an important vision of reality depicted by a prominent French existentialist.

Bridge to Terabithia
by Katherine Paterson
New York: HarperCollins Children's Books, 1987

This popular novel, geared toward the intermediate grades, lends itself to a discussion of friendship, the search for the self, gender discrimination, and the nature of death. A fourth-grade boy deals with his feelings of not measuring up to his family's expectations, his learning to accept the friendship of a girl, and appreciating the role of fantasy in life.

Roll of Thunder, Hear My Cry
by Mildred D. Taylor
New York: Puffin Reprint, 1997

Set in the Depression-era South, this novel contains many memorable scenes depicting racial inequities. The central African American characters are a farm family trying to survive, both socially and economically. An especially powerful scene describes young "Little Man's" anger at being forced to accept discarded textbooks from the White school. Issues of dignity, fairness, poverty, "right" behavior, and racial tensions are explored.

Izzy Willy Nilly
by Cynthia Voigt
New York: Aladdin Paperbacks, 1995

The heroine is a popular teenager until she loses a leg in an accident. The nature of friendship is a strong element in this novel, as well as dealing with the hardships of life. When Izzy experiences her loss, she questions how well her family and friends understand how she feels.

Harry Potter and the Sorcerer's Stone
by J. K. Rowling
New York: Scholastic Inc., 1997

On the surface of things, young Harry Potter is a future wizard, not a philosopher. But the world he inhabits is fully inflected with philosophical concepts, puzzles, and paradoxes. All it takes is a short step back from the vivid characterizations and intricately wrought plot to appreciate the mystery and wonder that surround Harry and his youthful cohorts as they learn the fine art of becoming wizards and witches at Hogwarts School. Questions in ethics (Is power more important than good?), epistemology (How can we know ghosts and trolls?), metaphysics (How do spells work?), and many more quandaries of this sort are natural responses to this excellent work of fiction. Pursuing these questions in a philosophical way will not interfere in the least with participating in Harry's wizardly and wondrous world!

Fahrenheit 451
By Ray Bradbury
New York: Ballantine, 1953

Science fiction affords a rich field for philosophical thought, and this well-known classic is an especially fertile source. Questions about the effects of technology, the nature of happiness, the importance of emotions, the status of the outsider (the "book people"), and the crucial relevance of simply being in a position to know about and question ideas are just some of the issues that arise in a stark and dramatic way from this book.

Where the Sidewalk Ends
By Shel Silverstein
New York: HarperCollins, 1974.

These quirky and occasionally somber poems go directly to that region in the spirit of young people where they do their most private—and profound—thinking. *Saturday Review* said that the poems are "tender, funny, sentimental, philosophical, and ridiculous in turn, and they're for all ages." Recommended for evoking aspects of young people's experience that intersect with philosophical concerns: values, friendship, and what is real beyond the point "where the sidewalk ends."

Glossary

The definitions of the following terms apply primarily to the discussions in *Philosophy for Kids*. Several terms are controversial (e.g., "meaning," "reason," "truth") and, as such, would be defined in various ways by philosophers. Also, any term that appears in bold in a definition has its own entry in the Glossary. Note: When appropriate, questions in *Philosophy for Kids* in which a term is especially important will be indicated at the end of the definition of that term.

aphorism: a concise, short **proposition** intended to state a **truth**. (See **Question #3**.)

argument: the basic structure of reasoning—a **premiss** (or premisses) leading to a **conclusion**.

AI (artificial intelligence): the discipline that describes and analyzes the functions of computers and similar machines with respect to whether these functions resemble human intelligence. (See **Question #20**.)

assumption: a **proposition** (or propositions) that a philosopher accepts as "given," that is, it does not require proof before being employed in reasoning and in the formulation of a **theory**.

"Big Bang" Theory: the **theory** in **cosmology** that asserts that the universe began about 20 billion years ago from an explosion of a small amount of matter of high density and temperature. (See **Question #26**.)

class: a group of things sharing the same characteristic (as in the class of trees). Classes are the primary elements of some types of **proposition**. Thus, in the proposition *Some trees are tall,* trees represent one class and tall (things) represent another class.

concept:	the basic element of thinking and reasoning. A concept is an idea, understood in an extremely broad sense, that the mind is capable of conceiving. Thus, "justice," "friendship," "effort," and "time" are all examples of concepts. Philosophers devote considerable time to analyzing the meaning of concepts.
conclusion:	in **logic**, the result of reasoning through a **premiss** (or premisses); the point stated as a **proposition** that an **argument** is intended to show. (See **Question #39**.)
contradiction:	a **proposition** that is necessarily false. Thus, "*This ball is red*" and "*This ball is not red*" are propositions that, if combined into "*This ball is red and this ball is not red*" produce a contradiction.
cosmology:	the philosophical study of the structure of the universe (or "cosmos"). (See **Question #26**.)
counterexample:	an example that satisfies the stated conditions of a **definition** in such a way as to show that the definition is false or incomplete. (See **Question #1**.)
critical thinking:	the branch of **philosophy** (and **logic**) that analyzes how to evaluate reasoning or any discussion that attempts to demonstrate a **conclusion**. (See **Questions #31–#40**.)
definition:	an account of a **concept** that states the nature or **meaning** of that concept. (Four types of definition are discussed in **Question #40**.)
distinction:	analyzing or dividing a complex **concept** into smaller or more easily understood parts. Thus, justice may be distinguished into *individual* justice and *social* justice, depending on whether justice concerns one individual interacting with another individual or whether it concerns an entire **class** of people.
end:	the intended (or, at times, unintended) result of a natural process or an action. To be contrasted with **means**. For example, the end of an acorn is to become an oak tree; the intended end of participating in a peace march is to produce social justice.

epistemology: the branch of **philosophy** that studies how we know. (See **Questions #11–#20.**)

ethics: the branch of **philosophy** that studies values, what we believe to be important in life. (See **Questions #1–#10.**)

existentialism: the movement in 20th-century philosophy that emphasized concrete or practical aspects of human "existence." Martin Heidegger (**Question #10**) and Jean-Paul Sartre (**Question #18**) are usually classified as existentialists.

fallacy: an incorrect pattern of reasoning. (Examples of informal fallacies are discussed in **Questions #33, #35, #36**, and **#37.**)

knowledge: names a state of mind in which we are objectively certain of states of affairs, or facts, in the world. (See especially **Question #16**, as well as the other questions in Part II.)

language game: the philosopher Ludwig Wittgenstein's name for describing how language functions and is meaningful according to certain set rules that govern the combination of words in sentences. (See **Question #17.**)

logic: the study of correct and incorrect reasoning in terms of its formal structure, rather than its content. (See **Question #39.**)

materialism: the **theory** in **metaphysics** that maintains that reality exists only as states or combinations of matter. (See **Question #22.**)

meaning: the significance or sense of a **proposition**; to be distinguished from the **reference** aspect of propositions.

means: the methods or ways of achieving a certain result; to be contrasted with **end**. Thus, holding a peace march is a means intended to produce a certain end.

metaphysics: the branch of **philosophy** that describes and analyzes reality by reasoning with general and abstract concepts. (See **Questions #21–#30.**)

paradox: understood in a popular way, something that is mysterious or difficult to comprehend. A more rigorous definition is a **proposition** that produces results that appear to be a **contradiction**. (For two different examples of philosophical paradoxes, see **Questions #11**and **#38**.)

perception: the process of becoming conscious of what we can sense both internally about ourselves and externally about everything that is outside ourselves. (See **Question #14** and **#19**.)

philosophy: literally, the "love of wisdom," wanting to understand and to be wise about as much of the world and oneself as is humanly possible. (See any question in this book!)

premiss: the **proposition** or propositions of an **argument** that provide information and reasons to justify drawing a **conclusion** in that argument.

principle: a set of fundamental concepts from which a **theory** can be produced.

proposition: the basic linguistic unit conveying **meaning** in an **argument**. A proposition is usually equivalent to a declarative sentence (e.g., "*It is a duty to give to charity*" is a proposition).

reason: what we do when we combine a **premiss** or premisses in order to establish a **conclusion**. (See **Question #39**.)

reference: the name for what a **proposition** points to or indicates. Thus the proposition *"All philosophers are happy"* refers to the class of all philosophers; to be contrasted with **meaning**. (See **Questions #21** and **#38**.)

refutation: to refute a theoretical position is to demonstrate through reasoning or through a **counterexample** that a given philosophical position or **definition** is false. (See **Question #1** and **Question #33**.)

stoicism: the position in **ethics** that emphasizes indifference to pleasure or pain or any "creature comforts." (See **Question #4**.)

theology: the theoretical study of the existence and nature of God and of religious and philosophical concepts pertaining to God.

theory: an account of some aspect of reality based on assumptions and principles and using observation and reasoning. Thus, one explanation of the origin of the universe is the **Big Bang theory**.

truth: according to one **theory**, the correspondence between a **proposition** and a fact about the world. Thus, the proposition "The cat is on the mat" is true if it is a demonstrated fact that the cat is on the mat. (See **Question #12**. For an alternate theory of truth, see **Question #29**.)

utilitarianism: the name of the position in **ethics** that maintains that happiness is (a) pleasure and the absence of pain and (b) the greatest good for the greatest number of people. (See **Question #6**.)

validity: in **logic**, when the premises of an argument necessarily lead to or imply the **conclusion**. (See **Question #39**.)

Index

195

Index

About the Author

David A. White has a doctorate in philosophy from the University of Toronto and has taught philosophy in colleges and universities since 1967. He has written six books and over 50 articles in philosophy, literary criticism, and educational theory (including an ongoing series of articles on philosophy and gifted students in *Gifted Child Today*). In 1985, he received a Fellowship from the American Council of Learned Societies to study the function of myth in Plato's philosophy. Since 1993, he has taught programs in philosophy for the gifted centers and various magnet schools of the Chicago Public School system, the International Baccalaureate program at Lincoln Park High School in Chicago and Northwestern University's Center for Talent Development, grades 4–9. Dr. White is an adjunct associate professor in the philosophy department of DePaul University and also teaches for DePaul's American Studies program. David is married to a philosopher, Mary Jeanne Larrabee, and has two sons, Daniel and Colin, both of whom are much smarter than he is.

"Philosophy is at bottom home-sickness—the longing to be at home everywhere."
Friedrich Novalis, poet